MACMILLAN MODERN NOVELISTS

General Editor: Norman Page

UNIVERSITY OF GLAMORGAN
LEARNING RESOURCES CENTRE

Pontypridd, Mid Glamorgan, CF37 1DL
Telephone: Pontypridd (01443) 482626

MACMILLAN MODERN NOVELISTS

Published titles
ALBERT CAMUS   Philip Thody
FYODOR DOSTOEVSKY   Peter Conradi
WILLIAM FAULKNER   David Dowling
GUSTAVE FLAUBERT   David Roe
E. M. FORSTER   Norman Page
WILLIAM GOLDING   James Gindin
GRAHAM GREENE   Neil McEwan
CHRISTOPHER ISHERWOOD   Stephen Wade
HENRY JAMES   Alan Bellringer
JAMES JOYCE   Richard Brown
D. H. LAWRENCE   G. M. Hyde
ROSAMOND LEHMANN   Judy Simons
DORIS LESSING   Ruth Whittaker
MALCOLM LOWRY   Tony Bareham
THOMAS MANN   Martin Travers
GEORGE ORWELL   Valerie Meyers
ANTHONY POWELL   Neil McEwan
MARCEL PROUST   Philip Thody
BARBARA PYM   Michael Cotsell
JEAN-PAUL SARTRE   Philip Thody
SIX WOMEN NOVELISTS   Merryn Williams
MURIEL SPARK   Norman Page
JOHN UPDIKE   Judie Newman
EVELYN WAUGH   Jacqueline McDonnell
H. G. WELLS   Michael Draper
VIRGINIA WOOLF   Edward Bishop

Forthcoming titles
MARGARET ATWOOD   Coral Ann Howells
SAUL BELLOW   Peter Hyland
IVY COMPTON-BURNETT   Janet Godden
JOSEPH CONRAD   Owen Knowles
GEORGE ELIOT   Alan Bellringer
F. SCOTT FITZGERALD   John Whitley
JOHN FOWLES   James Acheson
ERNEST HEMINGWAY   Peter Messent
NORMAN MAILER   Michael Glenday
V. S. NAIPAUL   Bruce King
PAUL SCOTT   G. K. Das
PATRICK WHITE   Mark Williams

MACMILLAN MODERN NOVELISTS

ROSAMOND LEHMANN

Judy Simons

MACMILLAN

First published 1992

Published by
MACMILLAN EDUCATION LTD
Houndmills, Basingstoke, Hampshire RG21 2XS
and London
Companies and representatives
throughout the world

Typeset by Nick Allen/Longworth Editorial Services
Longworth, Oxon.
Printed in Hong Kong

ISBN 0–333–53873–0 hardcover
ISBN 0–333–53874–9 paperback

A catalogue record for this book is available from the British Library.

Series Standing Order

If you would like to receive future titles in this series as they are published,
you can make use of our standing order facility. To place a standing order
please contact your bookseller or, in case of difficulty, write to us at the
address below with your name and address and the name of the series. Please
state with which title you wish to begin your standing order. (If you live
outside the United Kingdom we may not have the rights for your area, in
which case we will forward your order to the publisher concerned.)

Customer Services Department, Macmillan Distribution Ltd
Houndmills, Basingstoke, Hampshire, RG21 2XS, England.

To Juliet

Contents

Acknowledgements

The author and publishers wish to thank the Society of Authors, the literary representatives of the Estate of Rosamond Lehmann, for their kind permission for the use of copyright material.

Every effort has been made to trace all copyright holders, but if any have been overlooked the publishers will be pleased to make the necessary arrangement at the first opportunity.

General Editor's Preface

The death of the novel has often been announced, and part of the secret of its obstinate vitality must be its capacity for growth, adaptation, self-renewal and self-transformation: like some vigorous organism in a speeded-up Darwinian ecosystem, it adapts itself quickly to a changing world. War and revolution, economic crisis and social change, radically new ideologies such as Marxism and Freudianism, have made this century unprecedented in human history in the speed and extent of change, but the novel has shown an extraordinary capacity to find new forms and techniques and to accommodate new ideas and conceptions of human nature and human experience, and even to take up new positions on the nature of fiction itself.

In the generations immediately preceding and following 1914, the novel underwent a radical redefinition of its nature and possibilities. The present series of monographs is devoted to the novelists who created the modern novel and to those who, in their turn, either continued and extended, or reacted against and rejected, the traditions established during that period of intense exploration and experiment. It includes a number of those who lived and wrote in the nineteenth century but whose innovative contribution to the art of fiction makes it impossible to ignore them in any account of the origins of the modern novel; it also includes the so-called 'modernists' and those who in the mid- and late twentieth century have emerged as outstanding practitioners of this genre. The scope is, inevitably, international; not only, in the migratory and exile-haunted world of our century, do writers refuse to heed national frontiers – 'English' literature lays claim to Conrad the Pole, Henry James the American, and Joyce the

Irishman – but geniuses such as Flaubert, Dostoevsky and Kafka have had an influence on the fiction of many nations.

Each volume in the series is intended to provide an introduction to the fiction of the writer concerned, both for those approaching him or her for the first time and for those who are already familiar with some parts of the achievement in question and now wish to place it in the context of the total *oeuvre*. Although essential information relating to the writer's life and times is given, usually in an opening chapter, the approach is primarily critical and the emphasis is not upon 'background' or generalisations but upon close examination of important texts. Where an author is notably prolific, major texts have been made to convey, more summarily, a sense of the nature and quality of the author's work as a whole. Those who want to read further will find suggestions in the select bibliography included in each volume. Many novelists are, of course, not only novelists but also poets, essayists, biographers, dramatists, travel writers and so forth; many have practised shorter forms of fiction; and many have written letters or kept diaries that constitute a significant part of their literary output. A brief study cannot hope to deal with all these in detail, but where the shorter fiction and the non-fictional writings, public and private, have an important relationship to the novels, some space has been devoted to them.

NORMAN PAGE

1
Life and Background

Passionate and intelligent, beautiful and gifted, warm, vital and responsive, Rosamond Lehmann resembled nothing so much as one of her own heroines. Her life story is told in oblique ways throughout her successive fictions of womanhood as they map out the territory for an expanding feminine consciousness on its journey of development through the twentieth century. It is always dangerous to try to draw exact correspondences between an author's life and work, but the autobiographical basis of much of Lehmann's writing is undeniable. As she remarked in old age,

> so much of my 'life story' has gone, in various intricate disguises, and transmuted almost beyond my own recognition into my novels, that it would be difficult if not impossible to disentangle 'true' from 'not true'; declare 'This is pure invention, this partly happened, this very nearly happened, this did happen' – even if I could conceive it to be a worth-while operation.[1]

From the childhood episodes of her short stories and the evocation of adolescent awkwardness in *Invitation to the Waltz* to the exhilarating discovery of university life and the first raptures and disappointments of romance that occupy *Dusty Answer*, readers embark on a guided tour of Lehmann's own emotional career. Its turbulence is evoked in the intensely realised relationships of her novels, the paralysed polite marriage in *A Note in Music*, the overwhelming and hopeless love-affair in *The Weather in the Streets*, and the bitter lusts and jealousies of *The Ballad and the Source* and *The Echoing Grove*. Lehmann's artistic reputation has

1

been based on her creation of a distinctively female internal landscape, complex and fraught with anxieties. Frequently her
heroines undergo crises that parallel climactic stages in
Lehmann's own experience, and, as they struggle to understand
the nature of their own desires, they are simultaneously trying to
establish a grasp on the self that continues to elude them. Despite
her scrupulous analysis of the passionate lives of women,
Lehmann's own personality remains similarly difficult to pin
down. Poised and socially accomplished, she was also exceptionally vulnerable and her surface composure concealed violent
depths. As the poet C. Day Lewis wrote of her,

> A tranquil mien, but under it the nervous marauder
> Slithering from covert, a catspaw from a calm:
> Heaven's city adored in the palm of a pictured saint:
> My vision's *ara coeli*, my lust's familiar
> All hours, moods, shapes, desires that yield, elude, disarm –
>
> All woman she was.[2]

The contradictions and confusions that confront the protagonists
of Rosamond Lehmann's fiction reflect, however, not only the
vicissitudes of her personal fortunes but also the political and
social upheaval of the times in which she lived. Her life spanned
almost the entire twentieth century and her major work was produced during the period framed by two world wars. Her own
development was inevitably affected by large-scale world events
which early shocked her into recognising the precarious basis of
her social and cultural assumptions, and as she grew up, this
sense of life's unreliability became deeply engrained into her consciousness. Her work is grounded in insecurity and her heroines
yearn for commitment and stability only to find their ideals
broken and their confidence shattered. Lehmann's sensitivity to
her times and her acute political awareness are fused with her
insight into the personal lives of women caught up in the
processes of history, and one of her major achievements as a
novelist is the way in which she explores the response of individuals to the cultural shift of the age.

Born on the day of Queen Victoria's funeral, 3 February 1901, Rosamond Lehmann observed jokingly that the coincidence 'seemed to give an unexpectedly distinguished cachet: almost the reflection of a royal nimbus' to her birth.[3] More significantly, her birth date can be seen as marking the beginning of a new era. So the woman whose first novel was hailed by some as representing the voice of modern youth arrived in the world just as the one whose name denoted the values of the old age was leaving it. Certainly the 'royal nimbus' might well have seemed to have had its effect on Rosamond Lehmann's life. She was born into an unusually privileged and exceptionally talented family. Her father, Rudolph Lehmann, was a writer, a poet, contributor to and later editor of *Punch*, the humorous weekly magazine that for many people could be taken to embody the quintessence of Englishness. He was also a Liberal MP and a distinguished oarsman, a Cambridge Blue and coach to the Cambridge rowing crew, described by the young Teddy Roosevelt as 'about the greatest authority on rowing in the world'.[4] Rosamond's mother was Alice Davis, an American woman from New England and a graduate of Radcliffe College. She had met Rudolph Lehmann during his stay in Boston, where he had gone to act as coach to the Harvard crew, and where she was working as tutor to the daughters of a wealthy family.

Rosamond was the second of their four children. In her published collection of family photographs she includes one of herself as a baby in her mother's arms. Alice Lehmann is looking rueful. As Rosamond explains, after the birth of Helen, Rosamond's elder sister, her mother 'had hoped for a son', and among the congratulatory letters received on the occasion of the safe arrival of the second child are several that offered commiserations for Rosamond's not having been a boy. This consciousness of gender difference and her sense of failure to live up to expectations, noted so early in life, were to dominate Lehmann's writing in her delineation of the cultural and psychological distinctions between women and men. In *The Ballad and the Source* (1944), her fictional persona, Rebecca Landon, like Lehmann the second daughter in a family of three girls and a boy, bemoans the injustices of a system that privileges the male from the moment of birth, when her baby brother inherits a hundred pounds in a will from which his three sisters are omitted. Lehmann's own brother, John, reappears in Rosamond Lehmann's work as James, the quirky little brother, in *Invitation to the Waltz* (1932), a book that also presents a sensitive portrait of the complex and delicate relationship that exists between sisters. Indeed, family life, its subtleties, bonds and tensions, and in particular the experience of sisterhood, forms a pervasive subject in much of Lehmann's writing. The theme reaches its culmination in the intense analysis of the complementary jealousies and ties that link Madeleine and Dinah in *The Echoing Grove* (1953). But the complications of family life, the expectations parents place upon their children, the sense of mutual understanding that tacitly binds siblings together comprise a central focus of enquiry in both Lehmann's stories, such as 'The Gypsy's Baby' (1946), and in virtually all her major novels.

Rosamond Lehmann's own early experience of family life could by any standards be considered to be a highly protected one. She grew up at Bourne End in Buckinghamshire where Rudolph Lehmann had built a substantial and comfortable home, Fieldhead. The property had vast gardens stretching down to the River Thames and contained room in its grounds for stables, kennels, a boathouse and even a school, erected specifically for the Lehmann daughters' education and able to provide facilities for several carefully selected girls from neighbouring families, so that, as Rosamond Lehmann remembered, its complement of pupils came to about twenty-five in all. This house, sheltered from the intrusions of the outside world, provides the model for Judith Earle's home in *Dusty Answer* (1927), there resembling an enchanted but sterile place where a sleeping beauty grows up in peace and security before her awakening to the social and sexual reality that lies beyond. It was at Bourne End that Rosamond Lehmann spent her childhood years, with servants to look after her, other children to play with and a doting father who amused his children with inventive games and who encouraged his second daughter's clear penchant for writing. The house indeed formed the perfect environment for a budding writer. Portraits of great literary figures of the past, such as Robert Browning and Charles Dickens, who had been friends of Rosamond Lehmann's grandparents, hung on the walls of her father's library. Her great-grandfather, Robert Chambers of Edinburgh, had founded the *Chambers's Journal, Dictionary* and *Encylopaedia*, and Rosamond grew up with the consciousness of a formidable literary inheritance to live up to. Not that she found this a particularly daunting prospect. As she remarked in an interview given during the 1980s, 'There was a sense that I was bound to write. I never considered anything else a possibility for my future.'[5] As a child she had started to write verse from about the age of seven. Stories followed, precocious and often unintentionally comic. Yet, as she acknowledged, the act of writing gave her a degree of self-confidence and reassurance in her own identity that no other activity could match. 'I couldn't think what I was doing, quite, but I realised I was doing what I was born for. And then instead of being unsure of myself and often in floods of tears and feeling a strange despair, I felt I knew who I was.'[6] The compulsive nature of story-telling is a recurrent theme in her fiction. Imaginative children, such as Rebecca Landon in *The Ballad and the Source* or James Curtis in *Invitation to the Waltz*, are enthralled by the tales woven around them and by their own capacity to enter a world of fanciful projection.

Rosamond Lehmann's talents were allowed to flourish in the privacy and security of her home, watched over by her adored and adoring father. Interestingly, Lehmann's mother, Alice, figures little in the accounts of her early life. It is possible that the portrait of Mrs Earle, the elegant but distant mother of a sensitive, lonely daughter in *Dusty Answer*, owes something to her. Rosamond, a naturally nervous child, felt closer to her father, whom she greatly admired and whose influence on her development is evident. A victim of Parkinson's disease, he became increasingly disabled during her teenage years, a tragic physical deterioration that she was compelled to witness at first hand. As a child, however, secure in her home environment, she had no need to venture beyond the familiar territory and her education, from the time she was four until the age of seventeen, took place at Bourne End, on known ground.

The aura of childhood held a special place in Rosamond Lehmann's experience. Her autobiographical work, *The Swan in the Evening* (1967), isolates certain formative episodes in her early life, emotionally heightened vignettes that remained firmly

impressed upon her memory. The childhood scenes that occupy
the first section of this work appear almost as a series of photo-
graphic images captured in the moment of being and held as
self-contained tableaux. The pictorial analogy is one that she too
found useful in trying to evoke the quality of her recall,

> like a descent into a vault or cave or crypt, where all is dark-
> ness when you first penetrate. Then a torch flares, light is
> thrown here on a painted fresco, there on a carving or bas-
> relief: figures in a landscape, real and recognized, yet each
> with the mystifying impact of a symbol-in-itself, pure of inter-
> pretation and interpreter.[7]

Here are the impressions of childhood reviewed from the perspective of age. Informed by an understanding of suffering, of
loss, of death, they gain an added poignancy. In both her autobiographical writing and in her fiction, Lehmann is able to convey
the innocence of childhood without underestimating the intensity
of the emotions that accompany it. Despair, fear, rage, indignation
at injustice: these give the juvenile world its special fervour. In
her books childhood becomes a crucial determining factor in adult
lives. Several of Rosamond Lehmann's narrators are children, the
action of the novels they inhabit filtered through their impaired
but keenly felt vision. Judith Earle in *Dusty Answer*, Olivia Curtis
in *Invitation to the Waltz*, Rebecca Landon in *The Ballad and the
Source* manage to project the intensity of youthful feeling at the
same time as they are clearly fallible in their interpretation of the
complex adult entanglements that confront them. Yet the power of
their response to situations is not to be laughed away, and their
imperfect awareness contains a purity that provides an ironic edge
to the reader's perception. For children in Lehmann's work are
always to be taken seriously. The freshness of their insights,
while lacking the maturity of their later formed selves, offers an
original perspective on social existence. Lehmann's children
inhabit a world that is both secure and ephemeral. It is tightly
controlled by adult rules, by parents, by Nanny, by rituals of meal
times and bathtime. It is also a world whose innocence is inevitably due to crumble and consequently takes on a metaphoric
value in its enfolding of social and historical experience.

The degree of seclusion that Rosamond Lehmann personally enjoyed as a child was not as unusual then, for the daughters of the wealthy, as it would seem to us today. English girls' schools were not noted for their scholastic achievements and coeducational establishments were virtually unheard of. Certainly, whatever the social limitations, her education was sound enough for her to win a scholarship to read English Literature at Girton College, Cambridge, and in 1919 she left home for the first time to go to university. Life at Girton in the 1920s is described in the central section of Lehmann's first novel, *Dusty Answer*, published in 1927. Higher education for women was still relatively rare in England during this period, and the sexes remained strictly segregated. Girton, an all-women's college, imposed rigid rules on its female undergraduates. Girls were not allowed out late at night and male visitors were strictly forbidden, though during Lehmann's final year there rules were apparently relaxed so as to allow Girton inmates to meet young men for coffee in town – during mornings only. In *Dusty Answer*, Judith Earle's experiences at Cambridge are presented less in terms of the academic opportunities offered than in terms of her delight at being among other young women, free from parental restraint for the first time in their lives, absorbed in the process of self-discovery. The activities that form the bedrock of Judith's days have little to do with study, a matter acerbically noted by the novelist and critic Rose Macaulay in her review of the book. Confidences exchanged late into the night, boating parties on the river, drives into the countryside, and the heady stimulation of conversation with friends one's own age: these are the joys that Cambridge has to offer. There is in existence a photograph of Rosamond Lehmann, laughing with other undergraduates, as they pile gaily into a motor car, about to set off from Girton for a picnic. It forms a fitting complement to the picture of university life as she paints it for Judith Earle, her heroine, a life where the carefree pleasures of social excursions take precedence over tutorials, lectures or examinations. These more mundane events remain the province of boring swots, girls such as Mabel Fuller, the lower-class mediocrity who is forever barred from the privileged world that Judith accepts, not without some qualms, as her right.

Women who were up at Cambridge in that immediate post-war period also came into contact with young men who were starting late on their university careers, men who had fought in the trenches of the First World War. Older and more sophisticated than the conventional Cambridge student, they brought with them both the world-weariness of their war years and the determination to shed the knowledge of suffering they had prematurely encountered. The war had ended in November 1918. As the greatest conflict that Europe had ever known, it impressed itself on the twentieth-century consciousness so as to alter immeasurably the new generation's perception of life's meaning and possibilities. For those young men who had seen their friends shattered both physically and psychologically, who had watched schoolmates drowning in mud, and who had sent boys for whom they were responsible to their deaths, the idealism of the previous generation had permanently disintegrated. Nationalist fervour and abstract concepts of heroism were replaced by a new desperation in these men's re-formed attitude to life, a desperation that imbued their civilian activities with a sort of frenetic energy. The wild disregard for the past and the need to find a substitute in the immersion in the present moment appears repeatedly in the literature of the period as a phenomenon characteristic of the post-war generation. It is perhaps exposed most fiercely in Evelyn Waugh's satires of the Bright Young Things in *Decline and Fall* (1928) and *Vile Bodies* (1930). But it also surfaces in a number of books of those post-war years in the work of writers as different as Ronald Firbank and Virginia Woolf. Woolf's novel *Mrs Dalloway* (1925) is a particularly poignant evocation of the deep-seated damage the war inflicted on British society, in its concentration on the parallel experiences of a shell-shocked war veteran and the brittle social life of parties, charity bazaars and smart little luncheons that continue to form the fabric of socialite London. This ironic awareness of the duality of experience, in part a direct result of the aftermath of the war, is a fundamental ingredient of all Rosamond Lehmann's writing. As she commented, the First World War

cracked the whole structure of our secure, privileged and very happy life. The bath water grew cold; the huge lawn was dug up for potatoes, the sons of friends were killed. I became aware of grief – other people's grief, world grief.[8]

It is not only her first book, *Dusty Answer*, which conveys so brilliantly this equivocal sense of life's excitement and its corollary, suffering – though the portrait of Julian in that novel most perfectly demonstrates this dynamic of bitterness and insistent vivacity – but subsequent novels too are fraught with tensions arising from her profound understanding of the devastating effects of the Great War. Charlie Fyfe in *Dusty Answer*, Hugh Miller in *A Note in Music*, Timmy Douglas in *Invitation to the Waltz* and *The Weather in the Streets*, and Malcolm Thomson in *The Ballad and the Source* are all casualties of the cataclysmic struggle that left its ineradicable mark on the generation that succeeded it. The emotional ambivalence of Rosamond Lehmann's writing, that double-edged and subtle slippage between tragedy and joy, which for some readers became her hallmark, finds its source in this post-war consciousness first directly encountered by her during those Cambridge years.

In many ways Rosamond Lehmann was a typical product of Edwardian England, carrying with her the inheritance of Victorianism while welcoming the experimentalism of the new twentieth century. Profoundly aware of the value of tradition and with a respect for established mores, she could never completely repudiate the past in favour of current fashion. Her writing constantly demonstrates its debt to the past, both in its choice of technique and of subject matter, much of which concerns the power of history on both a personal and a global scale. At the same time, however, she was one of a new breed of women, enjoying a freedom of movement and expression that had been denied her predecessors. The First World War, as well as its tragic legacy of grief and the sense of futility it transmitted to the youth of the new age, had also effected radical changes in the whole fabric and structure of English society, not least in the ways it had altered a perception of gender roles and had opened up new possibilities for women of all ages. As the feminist literary critics Sandra Gilbert and Susan Gubar have noted, one of the paradoxical effects of the First World War was to upturn power relations between the sexes. The war, they suggest,

temporarily dispossessed male citizens of the primacy that had
always been their birthright, while permanently granting
women access to both the votes and the professions that they
had never before possessed. Similarly . . . artists covertly or
overtly celebrated the release of female desires and powers
which that revolution made possible, as well as the reunion (or
even reunification) of women which was a consequence of such
liberated energies.[9]

Rosamond Lehmann's writing indicates her own confusion at
being caught up in this process of upheaval. She had been
brought up to believe that girls should be 'pretty, modest, cultivated, home-loving, spirited, but also docile; they should chastely
await the coming of the right man, and then return his love and
live as faithful, happy wives and mothers ever after'.[10] On the
one hand Lehmann quite genuinely believed much of this. In *The
Swan in the Evening*, she acknowledges how the thought of a husband and family remained her ideal throughout her adolescence
and early twenties. Beautiful, elegant and well-educated, she certainly fulfilled the major requirements for the model young
woman of the day. But she was also intellectually independent
and had experienced a degree of freedom denied her mother's
generation. Like several other women writers of the inter-war
period, such as Rebecca West and Jean Rhys, her writing investigates the distinctive nature of female experience in this new
climate of emancipation, analysing in some detail the passionate
responses of her heroines and their attempts to acclimatise their
understanding of self to the society around them, itself under-
going deep-seated change. Lehmann's work is remarkable for its
exploration of gendered identity and gender relations, no longer
as fixed and immutable as they must have been for her forebears.
In Rosamond Lehmann's novels men are allowed to be sensitive,
weak, fragile beings, just as women are allowed positions of
strength and domination. Sybil Jardine, that magnetic figure who
holds sway over the lives of those around her in *The Ballad and
the Source* is in one sense a monstrous creation, a terrifying
manifestation of malign power, but she is also a woman whose
need for control is a defence against the injustices of the systems
that have conspired against women throughout Victorian times.

Her granddaughter, Maisie, in the same novel, is another prototype of a strong woman, this time of a different generation and
consequently able to choose her career as a doctor and her role as
a mother without the encumbrance of a husband. Similarly
Lehmann's fiction shows both men and women whose sense of
gender affiliation is by no means clear cut. Hints of homosexuality and lesbianism abound in her novels, even in characters as
apparently conservative in their lifestyles as Marigold Spencer in
Invitation to the Waltz and *The Weather in the Streets*. On the surface Marigold is the epitome of aristocratic respectability, but she
exhibits leanings towards her own sex that subvert the notion of
a fixed interpretation of her femininity.

Lehmann's own life at Cambridge and after brought her into
contact with a world of Bohemianism that must have formed a
sharp contrast with the sheltered and conformist world of her
home environment. Her new friends included a number of artists
and writers who adopted alternative attitudes both in their work
and in their personal lives. Although younger than the original
participants, Rosamond Lehmann was on the fringe of the
Bloomsbury Group and recognised the achievements these figures
had made in facilitating access to hitherto forbidden areas for artistic expression. In later life she retained a clear memory of
Virginia Woolf 'tapping me on the shoulder at a party and saying,
"Remember, we won this for you" – meaning the freedom to discuss sex without inhibition in masculine society'.[11] The Woolfs,
Lytton Strachey, Dora Carrington, Vanessa Bell and Duncan Grant
were all regular visitors to Lehmann's Oxfordshire home during
the early 1930s together with the talented youth of the new generation, such as Siegfried Sassoon, W. H. Auden, Christopher
Isherwood, Stephen Spender and Augustus John. Yet at the same
time as she was attracted to those who deliberately challenged
establishment values, Lehmann also retained close links with the
more conventional way of life that had always been familiar to
her. In 1923, shortly after leaving Cambridge, she had married
Leslie Runciman, a young man from a prominent, upright Metho-
dist family. It was a relationship that, as she remarked with
hindsight, was doomed from the start, lacking the dimension that
appealed to the ardent element in her nature. Her second husband,
the painter Wogan Phillips, more effectively bridged the gap that

opened between the upper-class society world of Lehmann's childhood and the artistic avant-garde she found so appealing. The tension between these two lifestyles is graphically depicted in *The Weather in the Streets* (1936), when the twenty-seven-year-old heroine, Olivia Curtis, finds herself in a similar predicament to Lehmann's own at a comparable age, torn between the correct and often comforting values of her family and the creative excitement of artistic non-conformity.

Rosamond Lehmann began work on her first novel, *Dusty Answer*, during her bleak marriage to Leslie Runciman. Although while at Cambridge she had written occasionally for *Granta*, the university magazine, she did not turn her attention seriously to literature until she found herself emotionally estranged from her first husband and removed from the supportive closeness of family and friends for the first time in her life. Shortly after their wedding the couple had moved to Newcastle upon Tyne where Leslie went to work in his father's shipping business. The sterility of the northern provincial town, as Rosamond Lehmann encountered it, is re-created as the setting for her second novel, *A Note in Music* (1930), where Grace Fairfax, the heroine, finds solace from the tedium of her daily life in romantic fantasising. Lehmann herself, similarly stranded, turned to writing for comfort, and *Dusty Answer* was the result. Having completed the manuscript, she showed it to a friend, George Rylands, who offered to send it to Chatto & Windus, where it was immediately accepted for publication. The book appeared in 1927 and made Rosamond Lehmann famous overnight, a fame enhanced by her personal beauty and society background. She was photographed for the *Tatler*, the fashionable British magazine, and the novel became an instant best seller both in England and in France. In the United States it was selected as Book of the Month by a leading book club, a choice that ensured her a huge transatlantic audience. The book's success could in part be attributed to its insider knowledge of the English upper classes at play, but it also seemed to represent the spirit of the new age in its portrayal of youth determined to grasp the moment of experience at its most intense. The sexually liberated climate of the novel accorded it something of a scandalous reputation. Together with the torrent of fan mail (which included a number of romantic proposals) came several letters that expressed outrage that a well-brought-up young woman should have knowledge of such subjects as free love and lesbianism, let alone display it to an audience. 'Before consigning your book to the flames', wrote one correspondent, identifying herself only as 'Mother of Six', '[I] would wish to inform you of my disgust that anyone should pen such filth, especially a MISS.'[12] This was a comment that Lehmann particularly relished and she was to use it again in describing the shocked reception to the publication of Sybil Jardine's sensational novel in *The Ballad and the Source*. Rosamond Lehmann's own standing as an author was much restored by the enthusiastic review of *Dusty Answer* written by Alfred Noyes for the *Sunday Times*. Noyes called the book 'remarkable', 'the most striking first novel of this generation' and, comparing Lehmann with Keats, stated categorically that *Dusty Answer* revealed 'new possibilities for literature'.[13] Several critics, however, proceeded to dismiss the book as a flash in the pan, a flukish first hit for a clever society girl, but in no way evidence of any lasting talent. During the next quarter of a century Rosamond Lehmann's work was to disprove such damning judgements. Although she was never as prolific as some of her contemporaries, devoting as much energy to her private life as to her writing, she steadily continued to produce work of increasing confidence and technical skill. By 1953, when *The Echoing Grove* appeared, she had published six novels and a collection of short stories, all testifying to her consistent growth in stature as a creative artist.

While living in Newcastle Rosamond Lehmann had met Wogan Phillips, the man who was to become her second husband. As the only member of the Communist Party who also had a seat in the House of Lords, he provided that blend of the radical and traditional that appealed to Lehmann's own contradictory leanings. They married in 1928 after her divorce from Leslie Runciman was made final. The couple moved to Ipsden House in Oxfordshire, a magnificent part-Elizabethan, part-Georgian building that had once belonged to the novelist Charles Reade. It was here that Rosamond Lehmann's two children were born: her son Hugo in 1929 and Sally, her daughter, in 1934. Ipsden soon became a centre where artists and writers could congregate in the atmosphere of warmth and hospitality that Lehmann seemed to generate spontaneously. Yet her natural grace and feminine charm belied her iron will and sense of artistic discipline, and her novels re-create this combination of seeming delicacy and intellectual vigour in their depiction of liberated heroines who also retain traditional womanly qualities. The description given of her during this time by the poet Stephen Spender suggests Lehmann's personal impact. 'Tall, and holding herself with a sense of her presence, her warmth and vitality prevented her from seeming coldly statuesque', wrote Spender in his autobiography, *World Within World*. 'She had almond-shaped eyes, a firm mouth which contradicted the impression of uncontrolled spontaneity given by her cheeks, which often blushed. Her manner was warm, impulsive, and yet like her mouth it concealed a cool self-control.'[14]

Lehmann's private photograph album from this period is filled with informal snapshots of the great literary figures of the day relaxing at Ipsden, from Virginia and Leonard Woolf to Ralph and Frances Partridge to David Garnett, the publisher of D. H. Lawrence. The milieu of devotion to serious artistic endeavour and to encouraging the avant-garde provides the basis for Lehmann's portrait of the artists, Anna and Simon, in *The Weather in the Streets* where she captures their quality of real originality as well as the suspicion with which such innovation was regarded by more cautious and conservative realists of the old school. While her admiration for the innovatory and experimental is whole-hearted, it does not prevent her from seeing the pretentiousness that creeps into the behaviour of less-talented imitators, and some of her most incisive attacks are directed at the notion of artistic preciousness. The portrait of the seventeen-year-old Amanda, precocious daughter of a wealthy patron of the arts in *The Weather in the Streets*, is modelled on the young Angelica Garnett, the daughter of Vanessa Bell and the niece of Virginia Woolf. Angelica might well have been 'lovely, graceful and surrounded by brilliance'[15] but the performance of 'original dances by Amanda' in the novel's coming-out party scene smacks rather too much of the indulgent approval given to any form of individual performance that calls itself art, however ungifted.

Lehmann's marriage to Wogan Phillips deteriorated and like her first was to end in divorce. At the start of the Second World War she was living alone in London while her two children stayed with her mother at Bourne End. By this stage she had become a successful and sought-after writer, giving talks on the BBC, contributing articles to literary journals and invited as celebrity speaker to literary meetings throughout the country. Although her sombre second novel, *A Note in Music*, disappointed those of her readers who had looked forward to a repeat of the effervescent mood of *Dusty Answer*, she had recaptured her initial popularity with the delicate comedy of *Invitation to the Waltz* and its sequel, *The Weather in the Streets*. Both works demonstrate Lehmann's range and her ability to shift between different literary modes. *Invitation to the Waltz*, perhaps her most subtle work, gains its effect from the impressionistic technique she describes so well at the beginning of her short story 'The Red-Haired Miss Daintreys', where an author is described as being

> a kind of screen upon which are projected images of persons – known well, a little, or not at all, seen once, or long ago, or every day; or as a kind of preserving jar in which float fragments of people and landscapes, and snatches of sound.[16]

The Weather in the Streets, although drawing on the same cast of characters as *Invitation to the Waltz*, is much more fervent in tone, presenting an in-depth study of illicit passion and revealing the unspoken suffering that a love-affair can contain.

In its range and scope Lehmann's work has provided a series of surprises for her reading public, coexistent with the turbulent nature of her personal life. From a knowledge of her sheltered and somewhat privileged upbringing, friends could have predicted a smooth untroubled future for the golden girl, a happy marriage – perhaps to a successful husband – and a gentle literary career as a pastime, unfolding without incident. The facts are quite different. Her first novel with its adventurous subject matter shocked her parents' circle of acquaintances and her subsequent work continued to explore the ramifications of social and sensual experience for women, its pleasures and its destructive power. Lehmann's satires of contemporary life are directed at every aspect of the society that had nurtured her. She spares neither the cultivated upper-class background that formed the context for her early life nor the progressive artistic milieu that applauded her talents. Her analysis of the confusions of identity in a changing society forms a consistent theme in her work, but her shifts of mood and of technique are continually arresting. Her private life was just as disturbing, containing a number of absorbing, passionate liaisons. Most particularly her relationship with the poet, Cecil Day Lewis, begun in 1941, was fraught with inconsistencies. Day Lewis's own marriage had already lapsed into an uncomfortable stalemate by the time he met Lehmann. With sympathy and understanding for his situation, she entered into a relationship with him that was to sustain her emotionally for the next nine years. She also involved herself in furthering his artistic development and career, providing him with an entrée to the publishing and literary world. As Day Lewis's son records,

> Throughout the decade when he had been the increasingly fashionable Poet of the Thirties, idealized by younger men of his kind, he had maintained his ascetic, outside, provincial view of the . . . stimulating competitiveness of fashionable literary London. Rosamond knew her way about this scene; she was at home with, and courted by, the grandest company, and she was able to coat Cecil's provincial inhibitions with metropolitan sophistication.[17]

Yet her commitment was to be rewarded by betrayal when in 1950 Day Lewis abandoned her to marry a much younger woman. Lehmann never recovered from this desertion. Her insight into the intensity of romantic involvement and the extremes of joy and despair such love-affairs incorporate springs directly from her experience of devotion and disappointment. In Lehmann's work the heightened pleasures of anticipation, so intensely evoked, are frequently overtaken by the pain of betrayal and the anguish of parting, features that are seen as the inevitable accompaniments to love.

During the war years Lehmann worked to commission for the first time in her career, contributing a number of short stories to the magazine, *New Writing*, which was edited by her brother, John. These were later collected and published together under the title *The Gypsy's Baby* (1946). This period also saw the publication of Lehmann's novel *The Ballad and the Source*, signalling yet another change in the direction of her work. This book focuses on the far-reaching effects of power through a study of one woman, Sybil Jardine, a dominating figure of immense stature who seems to tower over other Lehmann creations. The story is told through the eyes of the child, Rebecca Landon, a character who reappears in several of the short pieces written about this time and subsequently in *A Sea-Grape Tree* (1976). Its obsessive interest in story-telling as subject prefigures the post-modernist concern with the compelling nature of fiction and the processes of narrative fabrication. It was throughout this troubled and politically difficult period that Rosamond Lehmann's life was additionally complicated by her lengthy affair with Day Lewis. Although this provided her with an emotional reference point, its interrupted nature and its abrupt ending in 1950 had serious psychological consequences. It almost certainly provided inspiration for *The Echoing Grove* (1953) with its bitter realism of tone and its insistent analysis of the corrosive effects of love. A technical *tour de force* in its brilliant interplay of perspectives, this book also testifies to Lehmann's continuing interest in artistic experiment and her rigorous attention to narrative method. The familiar subject of the eternal triangle is given a new twist in this work as Lehmann proceeds to dissect the lives of two sisters, Madeleine and Dinah, and the painful and tortuous detail of their relationships with Rickie, the husband of one and the lover of the other.

The developing parabola of Lehmann's career as a novelist came to a sudden halt in 1958 after her beloved daughter, Sally, died of poliomyelitis in Jakarta, where she had been living with her husband, the writer, P. J. Kavanagh. Lehmann has said that she measured her life not by dates but by Sally, a life divided into three periods of time: before her daughter's birth, the duration of her life span, and the time after her death. The blow of her loss was so stunning as to effect a profound change in Rosamond Lehmann's attitude to life as a whole, her behaviour patterns and her approach to writing. Critics have remarked that she never again produced anything of literary value and in assessing her limited output since 1958 have treated it with kindly but uncomprehending attention. Certainly for a long while Lehmann could not turn her mind to creative production of any description.

Devastated by the news of her bereavement, she needed time and space in which to readjust the tenor of her life. She was to find an unexpected consolation in mysticism. As a writer she had always shown an interest in the workings of memory, of imagination and in the nature and processes of unspoken communication that exists between individuals. Her concern with the power of the past, with the ever-present impact of childhood on the adult consciousness, the ability of those who have died to make their presence felt forms a continuous thematic thread in her fiction. Grace Fairfax in *A Note in Music* lives in a mental world largely populated by figures who bear only a tangential relation to their real-life counterparts. In *Invitation to the Waltz* the dead overshadow the world of the living through ancestral portraits, photographs and personal memories. *The Ballad and the Source* shows a woman whose *raison d'être* is determined by the past and who is able to control others by the strength of an experience of which they are the unwilling legatees. Given Lehmann's continued fascination with these ideas, it is not as surprising as it might at first seem that she turned so readily to spiritualism as offering her comfort from the unreality of her life after the shock of Sally's death. She was to become Vice-President of the Society for Psychic Studies and together with Wellesley Tudor Pole, also a mystic, published a spiritualist work, *A Man Seen Afar* (1965).

In 1967 Lehmann returned to critical notice with the publication of her memoir, *The Swan in the Evening*. Her only attempt at formal autobiography, this impressionistic re-creation of selected childhood episodes placed them side by side with recollections of her daughter and her faith in their renewed contact. To many readers the shift of ground from Rosamond Lehmann's previous work and its deviation from conventional patterns of thought was unacceptable. A striking feature of Lehmann's writing from her earliest appearance as an author has been to make her audiences uncomfortable and to disrupt commonplace expectations. *The Swan in the Evening*, although very different from her first book, *Dusty Answer*, produced the same effect of displacing assumptions about what topics are acceptable for publication. Lehmann only produced one further novel. *A Sea-Grape Tree*, her last completed work, takes up the story of Rebecca Landon from *The Ballad and the Source* and explores in fictive form the power of spiritual contact as the presence of the dead Sybil Jardine continues to exert an influence over Rebecca's life and love-affairs. The conceptual basis of the novel, its assertion of spiritual links between the dead and the living, was suspiciously received and as Lehmann herself later remarked, as an experiment it was perhaps 'rash and courted irritation, head-shaking, even mockery'.[18] Clearly the figure of Sybil, a woman bound by the past and needing to exert her influence over the events of her lifetime and those of her successors, was one from which Lehmann could not escape. Even in her eighties she still had in mind the outline for yet another novel using the same set of characters, updated to the present day, leaving behind the world of myth and magic of *A Sea-Grape Tree* and returning to the realistic mode of her previous works. By 1985, however, she was running out of energy, that commodity that had seemed limitless in her earlier years. Although she could see 'the entire landscape with figures, static, waiting to be animated, woven into an organic pattern', the prospect of putting pen to paper for once daunted her.[19]

Rosamond Lehmann died in March 1990. Despite her relatively limited output, she had become one of the most distinguished novelists of her era. She was an International Vice-President of International PEN, a Fellow of the Royal Society of Literature and a member of the Council of the Society of Authors. In 1982 she was awarded the CBE for her services to literature. During the last two decades of her life, with the republication of her novels by Virago Press, she acquired a new following of readers, mostly women, from a generation whose mothers and grandmothers had been avid Lehmann fans. Her writing, although placed firmly within a precise historical and cultural context, embraces a sweep of experience that transcends social detail to speak directly to women who, although more liberated than Lehmann's heroines and with greater opportunities for personal and professional development, could yet find common ground in the emotional and psychic processes of which she wrote.

2
Women and Modernism

In *The Swan in the Evening* Rosamond Lehmann confessed to her early ignorance of developments in twentieth-century literature and of the modernist experiments being undertaken by women artists of the period. 'I knew no other female writers, young or old; with the exception of May Sinclair whose novels excited me',[20] she admitted, referring to the time when she started to write *Dusty Answer*. Yet, as she makes clear in her account of her literary development, she was deeply conscious of her own position within an inherited female tradition of fiction that reached back into the nineteenth century. Not Virginia Woolf or Katherine Mansfield, but George Eliot, the Brontës and Mrs Gaskell were the acknowledged literary giants who gave her inspiration, 'great ancestresses, revered, loved and somehow intimately known'.[21] Lehmann's novels demonstrate her debt to this tradition in ways that place her firmly within the ranks of contemporary enquiry, and we need to see her work within the context of women's writing of the period in order to understand her insistence on continuity as well as her sensitivity to change. For while alert to the advantages of formal inventiveness in art, Lehmann's work appears to reject the more sophisticated manifestations of the avant-garde. The satiric attack on futuristic art and artists in *Invitation to the Waltz* and *The Weather in the Streets*, for instance, suggests a sceptical attitude towards the cult of the new that dominated much early twentieth-century artistic production. Drawing deeply on the traditions of the past, Lehmann demonstrates rather her debt to those women novelists who were her predecessors, paying tribute to their achievement by developing the characteristic female subjects of the nineteenth century. At the same time her books offer a radical critique of patriarchal society as it has affected twentieth-century women and fully recognise the altered milieu in which her characters must function. Without prioritising the technical ingenuity that for many critics came to characterise modernism, Lehmann's work yet forms a part of the crucial questioning of patriarchal tenets that also engaged other women writers of her day.

The notion of modernism as it has been constructed by literary critics has traditionally been rooted in the idea of an artistic challenge to the nineteenth-century heritage. Ezra Pound's famous dictum, 'Make It New', helped to establish a revised hierarchy of literary value, whereby conventional artistic techniques were condemned as outmoded in the light of the new perceptions of the twentieth century. In fiction the concept of a 'natural' order and the reliance on logical sequence or conventional narrative plotting were replaced by self-conscious artifice, a complicated framework of arcane references and by heavily symbolic patterning, techniques that formed an implicit rejection of the classic realist approach adopted by those writers, Bennett, Wells and Galsworthy, whom Virginia Woolf had termed 'Edwardian' novelists. The idea of a world view based on a shared ethical system seemed no longer valid in a society where Christianity had lost its power and where new scientific developments in anthropology and psychology had helped to disturb previously received assumptions about normative value. The contemporary wasteland that they found in the post-war Europe of the 1920s could only, for some artists, adequately be portrayed through practices that replicated their feelings of disillusionment, uncertainty, rootlessness and loss of faith. Modernist novels were signposted by their experiments with the time dimension, by the abandonment of story as a focus of interest and by their revisions of conventional plot mechanisms. Characterisation in these works was dynamically affected by the impact of Freudian theory and the consequent displacement of the myth of the stable personality. As Virginia Woolf remarked in 'Mr Bennett and Mrs Brown', 'In or about December 1910 human character changed.'[22] By the mid-1920s, constant shifts in narrative perspective and the amplified depiction of mental and psychological processes to represent the unique calibre of individual experience seemed to have become standard devices in the repertoire of the 'modern' novelist.[23]

Critics' interest in developments in twentieth-century writing has mostly been grounded in an appreciation of formal textual features such as these as markers of a new consciousness that defined the age. As Malcolm Bradbury has observed, 'Modernism . . . is concerned not so much with revolution in the world, as with revolution in the word.'[24] In turn this has led to a particular view of literary achievement, using technical innovation as the authentic measure of the modern artistic sensibility. Apart from Virginia Woolf, whose name invariably appears as the token woman in any list of 'great' literary innovators of this period, it has thus been the male authors of the day, and particularly those who highlighted formal experiment, who have been taken as heralding the new-wave writing. Joyce, Lawrence, Forster, Conrad, Eliot are familiar names in the literary critical canon in a way that Mansfield, Richardson, West, Lehmann and H.D. are not. Bradbury's most recent book on literary modernism, for instance, contains Virginia Woolf as the only woman whom he considers to have made a significant contribution to the modernist movement.[25] As Patricia Waugh has noted, the valuation of modernism, both in its own time and subsequently, has been to a considerable extent based on the acceptance of the theory of impersonality: Joyce's artist-God paring his fingernails or on Eliot's much acclaimed artistic credos. The reaction of many women artists to this, their refusal to accept objectivity and impersonal form as the absolute criteria of canonical value has led to their marginalisation from the literary critical hierarchy. For women, whose grasp on a common cultural identity has always been more tenuous than men's, assert rather the importance of the subjective impulse and the appreciation of personal value-systems that can shake the patriarchal preference for apparent rationality and inorganic abstraction. As Waugh goes on to argue, 'masculine "impersonality" comes to be seen not only as superior, but as a necessary defence against the inferior feminine qualities of emotionality and subjective impressionism'.[26]

Thus the relationship of women writers with modernism has been at best tangential. As Woolf herself commented in *A Room of One's Own*,

If one is a woman one is often surprised by a sudden splitting off of consciousness, say in walking down Whitehall, when from being the natural inheritor of that civilization, she becomes, on the contrary, outside of it, alien and critical.[27]

It is an ironic comment on the assumptions of literary criticism that Woolf's achievement has so frequently been located in her technical ingenuity as the characteristic that brings her work into the mainstream of literary development. For Woolf, like several of her contemporaries, was concerned to convey the quality of personal, subjective and often distinctively feminine perception. Her fictional characters do not automatically share a common standard of experience, but are highly individualistic, and often alienated from a central cultural position as embodied by, say, Mr Ramsay in *To the Lighthouse* or Sir William Bradshaw in *Mrs Dalloway*. In these texts it is Lily Briscoe, the woman artist, or Septimus Smith, the shell-shocked survivor of the trenches, whose voices carry conviction, but whose vision of the world is interpreted as bizarre by those in positions of social and political authority.

During her most prolific period, the inter-war years, Rosamond Lehmann came into contact with some of the most talented writers of her generation, including Virginia Woolf, T. S. Eliot, E. M. Forster and Lytton Strachey. Yet she never became fully integrated into that inner coterie that had formed the original nucleus of the Bloomsbury Group. 'I am reading R. Lehmann with some interest & admiration', observed Woolf dispassionately in her diary. 'These books don't matter – they flash a clear light here & there; but I suppose no more. But she has all the gifts (I suppose) that I lack.'[28] Although after the publication of *Dusty Answer* and *A Note in Music* Lehmann became much more disciplined in her approach to her work and more conscious of the need to strive for technical perfection, she always maintained a distance from the extreme virtuosity of the avant-garde. Her novels instead cultivate a deliberately equivocal attitude towards the most progressive tendencies of modernism and generate an ambivalence that is poised between a compulsive need for links with the past and a participation in the changing world of the contemporary scene. Frequently the subjects of her novels address the whole issue of the power of the past and its impact on modern youth who might wish to reject it. The adolescent protagonist of *Dusty Answer* represents a distinctive type of new woman in her attempt to cast off outdated models of behaviour, but her search for independence is continually shadowed by the images of the previous generation she tries to discard. *The Weather in the Streets* tells the story of a woman who seeks to build a life according to emotional impulse but who is ultimately forced to give way to an established social structure that seeks to typecast her and to crush her individuality. *The Ballad and the Source* takes as its central figure an iconoclastic woman whose survival depends on being able to negotiate entrenched value-systems that are fundamentally inimical to her interests. Indeed all Lehmann's heroines must recognise the strength of the system they are up against in order to challenge it effectively. Their anxieties are complemented by Lehmann's fictional method, which combines a sensitivity to new expressive techniques (for example, in her experiments with chronology, her revisionary use of narrative perspective and her psychoanalytic approach to character) with a strong reliance on established literary precedent.

Lehmann's work rather falls within the scope of the enterprise of other contemporary women artists who, like Virginia Woolf, were intent on validating experience that had hitherto been marginalised and on affirming a qualitative difference between male and female reception of social experience. I do not wish to suggest that such writers were not rigorous practitioners of their craft, or that they were impervious to the cultural changes in the contemporary world. Rather their response to such change was manifested differently from many male authors of the time, and in particular they paid special attention to the related and complex issues of gender and of personal and cultural identity, as well as to ways in which artistic practice could best accommodate and reflect these. In addition they were sensitive to the idea of an alternative literary past, working within but also forming an implicit critique of the masculine hierarchy. 'For we think back through our mothers if we are women', wrote Virginia Woolf in *A Room of One's Own*, defining the problems besetting the modern woman author. 'It is useless to go to the great men writers for help, however much one may go to them for pleasure.' For a woman writer, 'the weight, the pace, the stride of a man's mind are too unlike her own for her to lift anything substantial from him successfully. The ape is too distant to be sedulous.'[29] Lehmann's own insistence on her links with the Brontës and Mrs Gaskell rather than with Dickens or Trollope reflects her need to see artistic continuity in terms of gendered models. The familiarity of plot and subject matter of many of Lehmann's fictional structures is by no means casual, but a central element in her artistic strategy. Several of her works offer variants on the motif of 'a Young Lady's Entrance into the World', the subtitle of Fanny Burney's *Evelina* and an important topic for women's fiction since the eighteenth century. *Dusty Answer, Invitation to the Waltz* and *The Ballad and the Source* all focus on the social and sexual education of their heroines, who are shown emerging from a cocoon of innocence into an environment that is simultaneously one of confusion and enlightenment. In this respect the novels replicate the structures of a number of classic female texts, among them *Jane Eyre, Middlemarch* and *North and South*. The reworking of traditional narrative patterns, crucially revised in the light of a twentieth-century consciousness, thus forms a bridge between Lehmann, other women writers of her age and those both of the past and in the future. In Rosamond Lehmann's work the staple ingredients of the nineteenth-century 'woman's novel' – the romance plot, the heroine of sensibility, the action of moral awakening – are critically reworked so as to invest them with a significance appropriate to the climate of cultural destabilisation that existed in England during this period. As Rachel Blau Du-Plessis has remarked,

There is a consistent project that unites some twentieth-century women writers across the century, writers who examine how social practices surrounding gender have entered narrative, and who consequently use narrative to make critical statements about the psychosexual and sociocultural constructions of women. For all the writers selected, the romance plot, as a major expression of these social practices, is a major site for their intrepid scrutiny, critique and transformation of narrative.[30]

Rosamond Lehmann's application of the romance plot to contemporary women in her novels testifies to her own deep
involvement in this female 'project'. Certainly her major works
find their inspiration in the age-old device of the love story, but
Lehmann's use of this conventional structure is deliberately
deceptive. For Lehmann, like Woolf and Mansfield, rewrites the
habituated conventions so as to expose the seductive quality of
the romance format, and by so doing reveal its political implications. In her very first novel, *Dusty Answer*, Lehmann allows her
heroine's fantasies about romantic fulfilment to be quickly ex-
hausted when Judith finds herself acting out stereotypical fictional
scenarios. The three men who figure as romantic foils for Judith
Earle in that novel correspond to three archetypal heroes from the
world of popular fiction: Roddy the rhapsodic lover of adolescent
imagination, Martin the worthy and solid boy next door, and
Julian the glamorous but dangerous seducer. In turn, however,
Judith finds each to be fallible, the women's magazine paradigm
failing to provide her with the realisation of her romantic expectations. Similarly Olivia Curtis in *The Weather in the Streets* falls
victim to duplicitous masculine charm in her obsession for Rollo
Spencer. Rosalind Miles has dismissed this novel for what she
considers to be its simple-minded acceptance of the romance
pattern. 'Strip the story of its fashionable fleshing down to the
bare bones', she suggests, 'and it is revealed as yet another saga
of sensitive girl versus romantic irresistible sod, the game that
was old when Byron played it. No matter how artfully done, it is
still the same basic formula, the romance as before.'[31] Yet the
conventional patterning that establishes the programme for the
first part of the story ultimately fails Olivia, who like other
women in the novel, still remains bound by its power. Olivia herself is a travesty of a romantic heroine, the 'other woman' in an
adulterous affair, no longer enjoying her first youth or beauty. In
this novel the fictive mechanism of the love-story is exposed for
its delusive quality, a myth that bears little relation to the cold
reality of women's contemporary experience. By the time she
came to write *The Echoing Grove* Lehmann had become adept at
playing with this basic formula in order to uncover its capacity
for disillusionment and its destructive potential. That book's vari-
ation on the theme of the eternal triangle, its sombre tone

probably reflecting Lehmann's own bitterness after the ending of her long affair with C. Day Lewis, presents the joy of love as a diminishing commodity. The description of the intricate relationships between the three main characters highlights rather the compulsive and consuming nature of passion and its disastrous consequences on the lives of those enmeshed in its tortuous strands.

In virtually all her novels Lehmann uses the mechanics of traditional romance in order to undermine the dominant cultural ethos. She is a classic exponent of what Rachel Blau DuPlessis has called 'Writing Beyond the Ending', the tendency of twentieth-century women writers to take the love-story beyond the limits of its conventional conclusion, which assumes an equation between marriage and personal fulfilment. Lehmann's heroines either reject the married state, as do Judith Earle and Rebecca Landon, or they find it unsatisfactory, like Grace Fairfax and Sybil Jardine, or they discover, like Olivia Curtis and Dinah Burkett, that erotic passion is uncontainable within the expected social parameters. Lehmann's rejection of these traditional narrative ploys reinforces her characters' sense of failure and loss of identity in a twentieth-century world. The modernist preoccupation with rootlessness and the vision of a twentieth-century urban wasteland emerges forcefully in Lehmann's *The Weather in the Streets*, a bleak emotional landscape that offers no future for women who refuse to accommodate themselves to the conventional female roles. The atmosphere of desolation and numbness that Olivia faces at the end of the novel adds an ironic dimension to the youthful vision of hope at the conclusion of *Invitation to the Waltz*, and by implication to the promises of fulfilment held out to heroines at the conclusions of countless previous stories. For ultimately Olivia is left irresolute, paralysed and unable to take action, alienated from her culture, forced to cope with the erosion of personal identity that her rejection of traditional cultural models has generated. Whereas many female modernist authors, such as Woolf and Mansfield, portray solitary women, talented individuals frustrated by their Edwardian upbringing, or resisting in subtle ways the expectations placed upon them by their families, Lehmann presents romance as a permanent imaginative attraction for women who willingly fall victim to its allure.

Consequently it acquires the force of a political instrument, for while love in Lehmann's fiction undoubtedly helps women to achieve a vital degree of self-understanding, it simultaneously undermines and confuses their sense of self, and limits their real freedom and capacity for personal development.

Rosamond Lehmann's examination of female passionate experience is also closely connected with her interest in narrative, and several of her books focus on characters who succumb to the potency of story-telling either as recipients or as performers. Grace in *A Note in Music* and Olivia in *Invitation to the Waltz* concoct fantasies that are more vibrant than the reality which surrounds them, and their imaginative life becomes for them a tangible source of emotional engagement. A central matter of modernist enquiry was the place and function of art itself, often perceived by artists of the age as a harmonising factor that could impose order on a chaotic existence. For women writers this search for a stabilising but creative centre was frequently identified with domesticity and the disclosure of artistry in hitherto unrecorded tasks. Mrs Ramsay in Woolf's *To the Lighthouse* creates a work of art out of her dinner-party, energising disparate elements into a unified entity. Mrs Fairfield in Mansfield's 'At the Bay' can transform a room through her arrangement of a bowl of glowing nasturtiums. Patricia Waugh has noted how,

> from Woolf, Mansfield and Stein to Drabble, Lessing and Atwood . . . women writers have typically explored human subjectivity and history in terms of non-systematized particulars, forms of collective expression, formal principles which suggest connection rather than fragmentation, history conceived as an ongoing human process.[32]

The interest in recovering narrative and the regression to traditional forms of story-telling related to this enterprise is a characteristic of the work of a number of modernist women, Rosamond Lehmann among them. Many of these writers emphasise the importance of oral narrative in women's lives, the handing down of tales from one generation to another and the permanent appeal of time-honoured genres such as fairy-tale and myth. Lehmann's *The Ballad and the Source*, in its concentration on narrative as performance art and its ability to draw characters into the drama of a past age, demonstrates the expressive capacity of collective art and brilliantly enacts ways in which women retrieve and utilise the fictions that they themselves have lived. It forms a subtle comment on the more schematic use of myth in, for example, texts such as James Joyce's *Ulysses*, where the use of classic formulae seeks to emphasise disjunction rather than unity.

The climate of artistic revolution of the early twentieth century allowed scope for women writers to make explicit the challenge to masculine hierarchies that, as recent feminist critics have demonstrated, had been implicit in many nineteenth-century female texts.[33] Dorothy Richardson, Virginia Woolf, Katherine Mansfield and Gertrude Stein all attempted through their writing to define a female aesthetic appropriate to the revised awareness of gendered identity that was an inevitable result of the First World War. It is significant that their work has frequently been read by the literary establishment as odd, possibly interesting but essentially slight, in part perhaps a natural consequence of its minority bias. Dorothy Richardson's revolutionary style, for instance, was originally termed 'neurasthenic' by one critic, a word that conveniently yoked images of women, instability and anarchy in the public imagination.[34] Yet for Virginia Woolf, Richardson's linguistic experiments, clearly challenging the concept of authorial impersonality, were also triumphantly associated with the attempt to create a uniquely female voice. What Richardson had invented was 'a woman's sentence, but only in the sense that it is used to describe a woman's mind by a writer who is neither proud nor afraid of anything she may discover in the psychology of her sex'.[35] Similarly Katherine Mansfield, a sensitive and vigorous analyst of the psychological repression of women in the patriarchal order, struggled, as her *Journal* demonstrates, to develop a literary mode that would effectively embody her personal artistic credo. Her dismissal of the ending to one of her finest short stories as 'a little bit made up' suggests her need to liberate her style from accepted conventions. 'I used them to round off something – didn't I?', she asked of herself about Mr and Mrs Dove. 'Is that quite my game? No, it's not. It's not quite the kind of truth I'm after.'[36] Because of Mansfield's refusal to conform to a standard artistic format, her work, belittled even by those who recognised her achievement, was denied status. Her conscious choice to work with the genre of the short story rather than the novel and her deliberately fragmented style were taken as seriously diminishing her scope as an author. It is significant that Rosamond Lehmann, a writer who provides an intensive examination of the nature of femininity and whose artistic method relies on a celebration of the subjective, has been similarly dismissed by the critical establishment for being so blatantly 'a woman's novelist', a designation clearly intended as pejorative.[37]

In their concern to establish a distinctively female aesthetic, women writers of the immediate post-war generation frequently concentrated on the portrayal of a specifically female subjectivity. As Mary McCarthy has observed, 'The fictional experiments of the twentieth century went in two directions: sensibility and sensation. To speak very broadly. . . . The novel of sensibility was feminine, and the novel of sensation was masculine.'[38] The attempt to convey the workings of the inner consciousness is, of course, a notable feature of modernist writing by men as well as women. As the concept of an axiomatic objective truth came into question, novelists generally abandoned the role of omniscient narrator and turned their attention to the presentation of internal experience as a more reliable means of conveying reality. Yet women's experience remained persistently outside the limits of the world that male writers could imaginatively evoke. Joyce's Molly Bloom, for example, whose voice takes over the final section of *Ulysses*, is an archetypal figure of male fantasy, permanently in bed, created only in a sexual and domestic dimension, in her roles as mother, lover, mistress, wife. D. H. Lawrence has become notorious among feminist critics for his fetishistic attitude to women, his female characters used to act out scenarios of male sexual fulfilment. Whether sensual creations like Molly or educated beings such as Ursula Brangwen, these women, however articulate, remain projections of masculine ideology and consequently excluded from the cultural superstructure, despite the apparently liberated dialogue in which they participate.

Women writers set out to redress this balance and did so in a cultural environment that gave them more freedom to revise their perceptions of self as well as providing them with a milieu alert to artistic innovation. As Gillian Hanscombe and Virginia Smythe have demonstrated in their study of modernist women, a large number of women writers of the period were as adventurous in their personal lives as in their writing.[39] Certainly Rosamond Lehmann, in the second wave of modernist women writers, broke with the tradition of her Edwardian upbringing in her particular search for emotional satisfaction and her refusal to accept the model of faithful and contented wife and mother that was held out for her. Her unconventional private life forms a natural context for her representation of women's sensibility and her investigation into what constitutes femininity in its psychological and social forms. For together with the enquiry into the psychoanalytical aspects of identity, which formed a central subject of avant-garde writing during this period, runs the complementary enquiry into appropriate social roles for women in a post-war climate that had effectively destroyed previously held assumptions about rigid gender division. Both areas of investigation were of course facilitated by the current developments in social and sexual psychology, by the publication in English of Freud's *Interpretation of Dreams* and *Totem and Taboo*, as well as by the work of writers such as Havelock Ellis. As Nancy Armstrong has pointed out, the new and more specialised language of the self provided by psychoanalysis in the early years of the century allowed women 'to represent depths in the female subject that were beyond the limits of an earlier discourse to imagine'.[40] By promoting the instinctual and irrational as central to their characters' responses, women writers presented an implicit challenge to the masculine insistence on order and control as determining a qualitative measure of experience. In Lehmann's *The Weather in the Streets*, for instance, Olivia is perceived by Rollo as a potentially subversive figure, threatening to break out of the category to which he has assigned her. 'I hope you're not going to do anything silly', he warns her at one point. In a novel that demonstrates the full complexity of social relations between the sexes, we see how Olivia's prioritisation of her emotional life jeopardises Rollo's safe position within the establishment structure, based upon reason and 'gentlemanly' codes of behaviour. Rollo's wife, Nicola, the embodiment of feminine debility, is quite acceptable within this framework because she is contained within the parameters determined by the patriarchy in a way that Olivia is not. Similarly in *The Ballad and the Source*, Sybil Jardine becomes an outcast from the tightly knit society that, as Lehmann effectively demonstrates, relies on male solidarity in its enforcement of law and order. Throughout the novel, women characters build connections, often based on tacit understanding of shared experience, on sensitivity, on tact and humanity that resist, though they are ultimately subject to, male control.

Woolf, Mansfield, Richardson and later Lehmann, through the extended use of represented perception, internalised their characters' experience so as to create women who were both recipients of a common cultural heritage and struggling to discover an individuality that could liberate them from the role models of the previous generation. The emergence of the New Woman, articulate, independent and educated, in turn-of-the-century literature, provided a prototype on which future writers could build, and which by the late 1920s had become an accepted feature of the literary scene. Lehmann's heroines are undeniably heroines of sensibility, highly impressionistic and keenly responsive to external stimuli. Their emotional intensity, however, by no means precludes their intellectual energy, and Lehmann's female characters, without being overtly feminist, are enlightened, sexually liberated and unafraid of the career possibilities open to them. Their inheritance is that of the First World War, the turning-point in changing attitudes to women, and when Judith Earle and Olivia Curtis go from their sheltered Edwardian homes up to university, their journey is one that in metaphorical terms takes them from one generation to the next.

Both the first group of modernist women, such as Richardson, Woolf and Mansfield, and subsequent writers, such as Lehmann, West and Rhys, in their social and cultural analyses, focus on the disparity between the public and private lives that women lead in order to suggest the discrepancies between male impositions of cultural practice and women's unvoiced personal feelings. Lehmann's division in *The Weather in the Streets*, for instance, between third- and first-person narrative serves to reflect these divergent aspects of experience: the received view of romantic passion and its disturbing subjective transmission. Her technical experiment falls within the scope of the enterprise initiated by

Dorothy Richardson and common to women writers of the time to transcribe the 'woman's sentence' and to re-create the difference of perspectives. So Richardson herself remarked that men and women cannot understand one another 'because they speak different languages.'[41]

Lehmann's presentation of Olivia in this novel and of her other heroines, such as Judith Earle, Sybil Jardine and Dinah, needs to be seen too in the context of the contemporary debate about sexuality. The genuine uncertainty that many women artists of the time felt about their own sexual allegiances transmitted itself to their fiction where female characters experience similar confusions about their own sexual psychology and the way in which this affects their social identity. Virginia Woolf's novels, for instance, not only distinguish between men's and women's linguistic codes, her satire frequently directed at the stagnant and hidebound structures of the English ruling class, but show both men and women who transgress strict gender boundaries. In Woolf's *Mrs Dalloway*, Clarissa Dalloway's recollection of Sally Seton's kiss in the rose garden is a more lasting and powerful erotic stimulant than her memories of courtship with either Peter Walsh, whose virility threatens to engulf her, or her husband, Richard Dalloway, who fails so utterly to move her. Katherine Mansfield's stories too investigate the blurred conceptualisation of the essentialist view of femininity. Beryl Fairfield in 'At The Bay', longs for romance and erotic awakening, her imagination roused by the images of popular fiction. Yet she is terrified by the potency of raw male sexuality when she encounters it and she is simultaneously exposed to and unnerved by the frankly lesbian gaze of Mrs Harry Kember, who watches her undress on the beach. This sort of situation is repeated in Lehmann's *Dusty Answer* as the heroine, Judith Earle, must find her way through a sexual maze, assessing her own responses to both heterosexual and lesbian impulses before she can arrive at a true understanding of her own identity. Indeed Lehmann's women, and several of her men, especially in the early novels, are frequently subject to desires that disturb their previously fixed understanding of selfhood. The boundaries between friendship and romance are often hazy – as in Judith's relationship with Jennifer in *Dusty Answer* or the intimacy that exists between Laura and Sybil, and later their granddaughters, Rebecca and Maisie, in *The Ballad and the Source* – and the affection of one can easily merge into the erotic dimension of the other. Indeed the language used to describe these relationships is sometimes virtually indistinguishable from the language of romantic encounters. Reporting the reunion of Laura and Sybil after a five-year absence Tilly, the maid is moved to tears. '"Five years," I 'eard one say; and the other: "I told you I'd come back". I see them sort of wander off into the drorin' room with their heads down, leanin' close, and not another word spoke' (p. 85).

The deep-seated sentimental affection evoked in this relationship blends with an appreciation of feminine beauty to suggest a more explicitly sensual dimension to female friendship. The attraction between Judith Earle and Jennifer Baird in a work that deals fundamentally with the intensity of adolescent ardour, is realised as a deeply moving and passionate experience that provides an episode of complete mutual absorption and emotional satisfaction in the lives of two young women at a transitional stage in their growing up.

> Always Jennifer. It was impossible to drink up enough of her; and a day without her was a day with the light gone. . . . But never forgetting Judith – or not for long; and coming back always to sit with her alone, and drop all masks and love her silently, watchfully with her eyes. (pp. 131–2)

Lehmann's novels all recognise the importance of passion as a central feature of the modern woman's experience, but the portrayal of female desire is by no means straightforward. Lehmann's heroines are unsettled by a mingling of their own instincts with their inherited assumptions about sexual codes and what has been instilled into them about the constituents of 'womanliness'. The new twentieth-century climate of sexual enlightenment, while allowing them the freedom to yield to passion, does not necessarily help them to gain any firmer grasp on their social identity. Women remain caught in a gender trap where their need for love and their personal beauty only aid their victimisation in a world of masculine power. The promise of liberation that is held out to Judith Earle at the end of *Dusty Answer* does not inevitably materialise for her successors: Grace Fairfax, Olivia Curtis, Sybil Jardine, Dinah or Madeleine, women whose sexuality is frustrated, exploited or turned into a weapon over which they have little control. Lehmann's heroines do not shrink from sexual experience, whether in or out of marriage, and it becomes a source of satisfaction often denied many pre-war fictional women. The fulfilment of desire, however, does not help to resolve the more serious question of how these women can arrive at full personal realisation.

The interest in female eroticism that forms a substantial element in all Lehmann's novels needs to be placed in the context of the wholescale enquiry that engaged many women artists of the time into the nature and scope of women's social roles. Most particularly, the emphasis on attachments between women, not necessarily sexual, often unspoken and frequently having the capacity to bridge generations, suggests the idea of a scheme of values and codes of behaviour that provides an alternative to the male reliance on legalistic, systematised models. As Virginia Woolf observed, a sentence in a contemporary novel, 'Chloe liked Olivia', signifies an immense change in emphasis in the direction of women's writing of this period. 'Chloe liked Olivia perhaps for the first time in literature', wrote Woolf. 'Cleopatra did not like Octavia. . . . And I tried to remember any case in the course of my reading where two women are represented as friends.'[42] What Woolf failed to find in the male literature of the past began to surface with increased prominence in twentieth-century writing by women. Several women authors record the mutually supportive nature of connections between women, facilitated by a mutual understanding of historical and social experience or by instinctive rapport that breaks down particularised barriers of age or cultural difference. Kezia and her grandmother in Mansfield's 'At the Bay' are absorbed in a tacit communion that binds them together in an intimacy that excludes all others. It prefigures the relationship in Lehmann's *The Ballad and the Source* that Sybil Jardine establishes with Rebecca, the granddaughter of her erstwhile best friend, and which as Rebecca comes to realise, represents for Sybil 'part of my grandmother she'd got back again' (p. 242). Through Rebecca, Sybil reaches out to the past to reconstruct a love that she had previously lost. Moreover the strength of such

relationships between women is frequently shown in the fiction of
the period to be more enduring than the power of heterosexual
attraction. Winifred Holtby's *The Crowded Street* (1924) shows a
heroine, who has been brought up to believe that marriage is the
only possible career for women, discarding the proposal that
finally comes her way because she has found new resources
through her friendship with another woman. In Violet Trefusis's
novel *Broderie Anglaise* (1935), two women who thought of each
other as rivals for a man's love discover when they meet that they
are on the same side, colleagues rather than enemies. Looking at
the other woman, Alexa, the heroine (a thinly disguised portrait of
Virginia Woolf), realises not just the contiguity between the two
but that her rival, by virtue of her femininity, is 'a link in an im-
memorial chain stretching back into the mists of time'.[43] Often
the ways in which women unite is found unexpectedly. In
Lehmann's *The Weather in the Streets*, Olivia discovers a submerged female network she never realised existed when she
becomes pregnant and needs to seek an abortion. Her cousin
Etty's sympathy for her plight springs from her own similar
experience, and the support she provides links Olivia in turn to
the women who had earlier helped Etty. This recognition of alternative routes for women has been linked with the aftermath of the
First World War and its effect on the restructuring of social and
sexual possibilities for women. As Sandra Gilbert and Susan
Gubar have observed, 'both the sisterhood and the sensuality
celebrated by such diverse writers as Holtby, Hall, Brittain and
Sackville West, fostered this vision of a world revised'.[44]

Despite her confessed ignorance at the beginning of her literary
career, her novels demonstrate that Lehmann was highly sensitive
to cultural and social change and to finding a method of fictional
expression that could adequately convey her sense of dislocation
from the mainstream of traditional culture. Her work testifies
continually to her awareness of the dominance of patriarchal
structures in contemporary society and the consequent powerlessness of women who wish to resist traditional roles. A significant
element in the presentation of the New Woman was her consciousness of her difference from men; while equality can be
legislative, economic and political, the difference remains an
essential factor in determining social relations. It is this crucial

difference that Lehmann explores. In taking on board the impact of psychoanalysis in the concept and presentation of personality, Lehmann's work suggests that identity is always culturally determined. Her examination of the cult of motherhood, for instance in *The Weather in the Streets* and *The Ballad and the Source*, challenges the fashionable notion that the mothering instinct is innate in women. Lehmann's mothers do not behave 'naturally' and her daughters do not automatically seek motherhood for biological reasons. But her enquiry into this issue forms part of a larger movement within modernism, for which gender was a locus of anxiety for both men and women artists of the period.

3

Testing the Water:
The Early Novels

On the surface Rosamond Lehmann's first two novels appear to be quite different in ambience and subject matter. *Dusty Answer* is a work that explores the condition of modern youth in a setting that is full of light and hope; *A Note in Music*, published three years later, focuses on the grey and spiritless atmosphere of failure. Yet, despite the difference in location and tone – the privileged and leisured rural environment of *Dusty Answer*, the cramped industrial north of *A Note in Music* – each work realises a post-war England that registers a sense of simultaneous excitement and disillusionment. The shift in fictional styles indicated in this early writing reflects the fluctuation between romance and realism that marks Lehmann's literary career. *Dusty Answer*, with its mood of youthful, heady eroticism, was an immediate success, but after the appearance of *A Note in Music*, Lehmann, who had originally been identified as a new voice speaking for her generation, was seen as having betrayed her initial promise in a work that was 'vague and undefined'.[45] Yet the pulsation between exhilaration and dejection that characterises Rosamond Lehmann's fictional world is established definitively in the oppositional modes of her first two novels. Although Grace Fairfax, the central character of *A Note in Music*, is a middle-aged frump, a startling contrast to the sparkling, adolescent Judith Earle of *Dusty Answer*, she can also be seen as a development of the earlier character, a dismal prophecy of what the future actually holds. And in their different ways, each book reveals Lehmann as a serious artist, a writer who, from the beginning of her career, was intent on literary innovation, both in terms of the subjects she was prepared to investigate and the technical verve she employed as part of that investigation.

Rosamond Lehmann's approach in *Dusty Answer* and *A Note in Music* is essentially exploratory, and the two books introduce a number of distinctive themes and interests that are developed with increasing power in her later writing. Each work focuses on an isolated heroine and the vividness of her fantasy life, establishing a meaningful contrast between the world of routine that she inhabits and the magical quality of the glamorous life elsewhere that she is permitted to glimpse. Whereas in *Dusty Answer*, Judith ultimately sees through and rejects this glamour, for Grace it remains an unattainable reminder of a world from which she is permanently barred. Together, these two women form the prototype of the failure of Lehmann's heroines to realise juvenile potential, seen subsequently in Olivia Curtis, the imaginative, eager adolescent of *Invitation to the Waltz*, whose gifts wither into inactivity. By the time she appears in *The Weather in the Streets*, Olivia's life is dominated by her sense of non-achievement, the brilliant career hinted at in the earlier book having failed to materialise. The theme is taken up again in *The Ballad and the Source*, where Sybil Jardine's early talents have been warped, and the course of her life redirected from a creative to a destructive path.

Lehmann's heroines in these first two novels express her own ambivalence towards the establishment structure. Like Olivia Curtis, who is their immediate fictional successor, Judith and Grace both present themselves as outwardly conventional, but both display an inner scepticism towards accepted modes of behaviour. They are unexceptional heroines, their radicalism private and unheralded, but in the impressionistic depiction of personal responses each suggests a longing to escape from restriction that could be taken as expressive of the malaise and the hopes of the contemporary generation. For both women display an extraordinary responsiveness, their sensibilities alive to the subtle implications of mundane situations, and in this they form the first examples of Lehmann's sustained examination of the twentieth-century female psyche. In their speculative approach to personal relationships, the texts indicate the uncertainty and anxieties of women's emotional direction. The delicate treatment of the relationships between Judith and the Fyfe boys, between Grace and Hugh Miller, between Judith and Jennifer Baird, illuminates the tenuous nature of the boundaries between friendship and love, and the strength of women's intimacy, both of which prove rich sites of exploration in Lehmann's writing. The innovative nature of these first two novels rests more on the adventurous nature of their content, particularly in *Dusty Answer*, than on formal experiment, despite the narrative permutations of *A Note in Music*. But it is *Dusty Answer* that was responsible for Lehmann's initial celebrity, and it is that work which most effectively illustrates both her fresh perspective on the contemporary scene and her links with a past tradition of women's writing.

Lehmann's daring treatment of her subject matter in *Dusty Answer*, with its casual assumptions about sexual experiment, does not conceal the novel's debt to its fictional past. The story follows the progress of the heroine, Judith Earle, during a crucial period in her life, the years from eighteen to twenty-one, and in particular deals with her fascination with a family of young cousins, the Fyfes, who since childhood have spent holidays staying with their grandmother in the house next door to Judith's own. The book is divided into five sections, each taking as its focus a discrete stage in Judith's emotional development. The opening recalls her childhood memories of times spent with the Fyfes, four boys and a girl, whose sophisticated London background has been in marked contrast to her own quiet country upbringing. In their self-assurance and ease of manner they have come to epitomise for Judith a charismatic world, and they provide a focus for the novel's theme of romantic disillusionment. The summer that Judith is eighteen the Fyfes return to the house next door after a break of some years, mourning the death in the Great War of Charlie, the most adored of the cousins. Mariella, now Charlie's widow and the mother of his baby son, provides an entrée for Judith to visit the family and to take up her early relationships with the three surviving young men: Roddy, Martin and Julian. The novel traces Judith's growth towards maturity, and in the process takes her through university life in Cambridge and depicts her passionate involvement there with Jennifer Baird, a fellow undergraduate, before describing the culmination of her relationship with the Fyfes. The closing chapters of the novel show Judith achieving a self-knowledge as a result of her experiments in love, and present her as a young woman ready for adulthood, with a sure sense of her own distinctive identity.

As this synopsis shows, the book's roots are firmly grounded in conventional nineteenth-century fictions of heroines and their quest for self-knowledge. Emma Woodhouse, Dorothea Brooke, Isobel Archer are the unacknowledged forerunners of Judith Earle – all privileged, intelligent, advanced women, who are none the less limited by the inevitable narrowness of their horizons. There are, however, a number of ways in which Lehmann's radical break with those traditions marks the work as decisively modernist in its concerns and techniques. The action of the novel, for instance, is visualised as a series of episodes in the life of the heroine rather than built around a tightly articulated plot. Correspondingly, the book's conclusion deliberately frustrates the notion of romantic fulfilment. It ends not with Judith's marriage to one of the eligible young men or with her awakening to the nature of love, but with her rejection of the romantic possibilities that have been held out to her. The whole portrayal of the central character is also very much of its time, insisting on the authority of the individual consciousness in determining the nature of events. Judith is an example of an essentially post-war woman with educational opportunities that were denied her pre-war fictional counterparts, even such liberated New Women as, for instance, H. G. Wells's Ann Veronica. These opportunities, which involve her leaving home at the age of eighteen, emancipate her both intellectually and socially. In addition, the relationships at the centre of the novel's action are presented with an explicitness that reflects the contemporary sexual revolution and its associated examination of gender. The book is in fact pervaded by a consciousness of the effects of the First World War and the changes that this has wrought in the lives of the young.

The portrayal of Judith, a product of a sheltered upbringing in Edwardian England, inevitably reflects something of Lehmann's own background and circumstances. Like Lehmann, Judith combines beauty and intelligence. Her parents are members of the wealthy intelligentsia, and Judith herself is educated privately at home before going on to Cambridge where she proves a brilliant

scholar. The setting for much of the novel is on the River Thames
where Judith's family home is situated, very similar to the
Lehmanns' at Bourne End. It is not merely through such bio-
graphical correspondences, however, that Judith's story resembles
Lehmann's own, but more fundamentally in the way in which her
life mirrors the world she inhabits as one in the process of
change, as she moves from her sheltered pre-war childhood to a
post-war adolescence virtually free from adult control. This tendency to remove the heroine from external guidance in order to
force her sense of personal responsibility was indeed a frequent
feature of many nineteenth-century novels. We have only to think
of Jane Austen's Anne Elliot with her totally inadequate father,
Charlotte Brontë's Jane Eyre, orphaned and cast alone on the
world, or George Eliot's Dorothea Brooke, forced into premature
independence, to recognise how familiar a motif this is in English
fiction. *Dusty Answer*, however, differs from these earlier works
in a number of important ways, for Judith seems to inhabit a
world where the young dominate and where parents, grandparents, teachers and guardians barely register as figures of
authority. Certainly, parents, when they do appear, are significant
figures who have a deep influence on their children's lives, but
the novel's emphasis is on the young. Judith's days in *Dusty
Answer* seem to consist of picnics with the Fyfes, firework parties, moonlight swims or of lunches in Cambridge, country drives
and talks lasting far into the night, when parents, conveniently
placed at a distance, are little more than useful bankers. Indeed
parents are mostly shadowy figures who are travelling abroad,
away in London or otherwise off stage. Consequently the world
of *Dusty Answer* is peopled by the same Bright Young Things of
Evelyn Waugh's satires of the period, a world where tradition has
largely been discarded as outdated by the new generation, and the
young are conscious of themselves as taking over a new, freer
post-war society.

Just as a number of nineteenth-century novels by women owe a
debt to romance models, so at the beginning of *Dusty Answer*,
Judith, beautiful and isolated in her empty house, resembles a
character in a fairy-tale who is unawakened to her own potential,
conscious only of her inadequacies in comparison with the family
in the house next door and quite unaware of how they see her. To

her their strangeness takes on an almost magical quality when set against the apparently prosaic routine of her own way of life. The Fyfes have the power to transform her entire being, her moments with them are spell-bound enchanted excursions into a fantastic environment. Charlie is 'a prince' (p. 13), Mariella 'a mermaid' (p. 9), Roddy 'reminded you of something fabulous' (p. 21). Even when grown up, the boys are no mere young men to Judith's eyes but 'giants in grey flannels' (p. 54). She looks to them for 'signs and wonders' (p. 27) and her times of joy spent in their company always terminate with a sense of finality as 'the mystery fell over them again, and they were as unattainable as ever' (p. 38). Theirs is a world of assumed superiority, not just in terms of their wealth and social background – Eton, Oxford and Cambridge – but also in their family closeness and their easy intimacy with one another, which binds them together as a unit and from which Judith, an only child, feels hopelessly excluded. This image of exclusion recurs in the novel each time she encounters a new group of people whose world seems closed to outsiders, the Cambridge 'set', for instance, with their private language and cryptic references, or the world of male companionship established by Roddy and his friend Tony Baring to which she can never be admitted. The experience of alienation is deeply embedded in all Rosamond Lehmann's fictions of women who feel like Judith on her arrival in Cambridge 'lost, lost, abandoned, alone, lost' (p. 108) in a bewildering environment that appears to be beyond their reach. Lehmann's heroines are desperate for acceptance into the precious coterie, whether it be the *jeunesse dorée* of Cambridge, the Fyfe's family group or the working-class children's game from which the middle-class child is isolated in 'The Gypsy's Baby'. It is a feeling that sweeps over Grace Fairfax in *A Note in Music* as she comes to realise her permanent exile from the world of elegance, breeding and comfort that she glimpses from within the boundary of her restrictive marriage. 'I don't understand a bit how to live with lots of people. I never have. I shall make such mistakes', Judith Earle tells Roddy Fyfe. 'It oppresses me, such a weight of lives crammed together in one building, such a terrifying press of faces. I prefer living alone' (p. 92). In following the process of female socialisation, Lehmann eloquently suggests the tension between the love of solitude and the demand for acceptance into a privileged community that so many of her heroines crave. And, as Judith moves from terror of others to an enjoyment of her growing self-confidence, so she learns the secret of social power, a subject explored throughout all Lehmann's fictional work.

Traditionally perhaps, Lehmann's focus remains the heroine of sensibility – sensitive, romantic and idealistic. In *Dusty Answer*, as in *A Note in Music* and *Invitation to the Waltz*, unfocused passionate ambition acquires definition as the novel proceeds, and in locating the narrative perspective in her heroine's consciousness the author creates a vehicle for conveying the inner processes and nuances of this development. Yet in *Dusty Answer* we are also asked to recognise the fallibility of the child's, and later the adolescent's, perceptions even at the moment when they appear most convincing. In reply to Judith's spontaneous childish avowal of love, Charlie says to her casually, 'I wish you were my sister'.

> At once it was clear that he did not really mean it. He did not care. He was used to people adoring him, wanting from him what he never gave but always charmingly pretended to give. It was a deep pang in the heart. She cried out awkwardly: 'Ah, you don't mean it! . . .' Yet at the same time there was a melting glow because he had after all said it.   (p. 16)

Later, when he solemnly gives her a pin he has found in his pudding at school, the child Judith is overcome.

> He was so beautiful, so gracious, so munificent that words failed. . . . She put the pin in a sealed envelope and wrote on it, 'The pin that nearly killed C. F.' with the date; and laid it away in the washstand drawer with her will and a bit of uncut turquoise, and some shells, and a piece of bark from the poplar tree that fell down in the garden.   (p. 16)

The imitative form of the simple syntax and vocabulary in this first section of the book recalls Joycean techniques in its dramatic rendering of childish intonation. The texture of juvenile experience is evoked in all its intensity, constituted of individual moments of vital sensation, both rapturous and painful, but always fleeting. 'If only the moment could stay fixed', wishes Judith later in the novel, luxuriating in the tranquillity of a picnic by the river where 'nothing memorable was said or done, yet all seemed significant' (p. 88). This evocation of transient fragments of experience is at the heart of Rosamond Lehmann's method in this novel and provides the foundation of her approach to presenting female experience in her subsequent fictions, where characters' lives are enacted and transformed in experience composed of passing moments.

It is through these glimpses into her childhood that Judith is realised as a passionate being, her responsiveness to others and to the delicate shades of experience remaining her distinguishing characteristic. She is also a sensual heroine, and her romantic idealism is accompanied by a very real awareness of its erotic implications. It is this that marks the text emphatically as a product of its time. Lehmann presents a whole series of incidents – swimming, climbing, skating, dancing – that attest to Judith's delight in her own physical prowess and the particular route for self-expression this liberates. The skating scene in the first section of the book is a perfect example of this, as Judith's freedom and confidence grow with her mastery of the ice. Her pleasure in the release of energy that skating embodies anticipates the *jouissance* to be explored in later episodes. Significantly, whirling on the frozen pond, she becomes the recipient of admiring male glances for the first time in her life. This physical freedom becomes more explicitly associated with sexual experience in the second section of the novel, where Judith, at the end of childhood but not yet a full adult, goes bathing. In a scene reminiscent of Kate Chopin's *The Awakening* (1899) where the heroine finds that the sea provides a symbolic complement to her libido, Judith swims naked in the moonlight, the highly charged language preparing the way for the later similar episodes.

It was exquisite joy to be naked in the water's sharp clasp. . . . To swim by moonlight alone was a sacred and passionate mystery. The water was in love with her body. She gave herself to it with reluctance and it embraced her bitterly. She endured it, soon she desired it; she was in love with it. Gradually its harshness was appeased, and it held her and caressed her gently in its motion. (p. 48)

The suggestive prose of this extract deliberately recalls a seduction scene, and the erotic tenor of the piece is heightened by the voyeuristic element introduced when it becomes clear that Judith's swim is observed by Roddy, the young man to whom she is attracted. Throughout the novel swimming continues to carry associations of erotic desire and its sublimated expression. Watching Jennifer naked at the side of a bathing pool near Cambridge, '"Glorious, glorious pagan that I adore!" whispered the voice of Judith that could never speak out' (p. 137) and on the brink of seduction by Julian, in the penultimate section of the novel, she finds in a hidden bathing-pool in a wide rock basin a metaphor of her own potential. The water is 'deep enough to dive into – if we dare break into such magic' (p. 264) she declares, as she hovers on the edge of sexual adventure. Bathing symbolises physical exhilaration and the body's capacity to explore the unknown, just as Julian offers Judith an adventure into new sexual, emotional and intellectual territory. Diving recklessly into the pool, Judith only just misses a shard of jagged rock. The dive provides a perfect image for her romantic relationships, characterised by her eagerness to immerse herself in passionate experience without considering the consequences. Lehmann suggests that personal involvement for women, exciting, though liberating and joyous, nevertheless contains unseen risks.

Just as Judith is adept at swimming and at skating, so she is a natural dancer, her physical being finding full expression in the rhythmic partnership. 'It was easier than walking, it was more delicious than swimming or climbing; her body had always known how it was done' (p. 70) she realises during her first lesson with Martin, and when she dances with Roddy, the man she has wanted since childhood, her initiation into the dance is described in language that deliberately suggests its orgasmic quality. 'Laughing silently he gathered her up and started whirling, whirling. A deeper dream started. The room was a blur, flying, sinking away; only Roddy's dark red tie and the line of his cheek and chin above it were real' (p. 73).

In plotting Judith's growth as one of emotional and sensual discovery, Lehmann develops a searching enquiry into the nature of femininity that becomes one of her recurrent themes. Significantly Judith's tentative romantic dreams about men are only allowed to flower after her Cambridge experience. For many of her original readers Lehmann's novel was the quintessential Cambridge novel, with the episodes depicting Judith's undergraduate career at its thematic as well as its formal core. *Dusty Answer* is probably the first English novel to deal with a girl's experience of university life, a rite of passage that at one stage in the later twentieth century seemed to become almost *de rigeur* for fictional young women needing to find their independence. In 1927, however, both the experience and its literary treatment were highly innovative. Interestingly the episode functions as a stage in Judith's emotional and psychological development rather than being seen as contributing to her intellectual and moral growth. The academic and scholarly life figures only as a background to the real subject of the Cambridge experience, the story of Judith's intimacy with Jennifer Baird.

Jennifer is a fascinating creation, a New Woman of the post-war era who openly acknowledges her sexuality and makes a feature of her womanliness. She represents an emancipated generation of young women of a type with whom Judith has had no previous contact, and as with Judith's early encounters with the Fyfes, so her first sight of Jennifer is an initiation into a new world. Jennifer smokes, swears, drinks, keeps herself fit with body-building exercises and talks openly about sex. She has enlightened parents and prioritises those aspects of experience that helped to contribute to the new aestheticism of the 1920s as promoted by G. E. Moore's *Principia Ethica* (1903). In accordance with this Bloomsbury bible, which elevated 'the pleasures of human intercourse and the enjoyment of beautiful objects'[46] to a high art form, friendship, personal beauty and *objets d'art* take precedence over academic work in Jennifer's life. More importantly, however, Jennifer functions as a projection of Judith's own nature for 'She was the part of you which you had never been able to untie and set free'(p. 137). Initially she is described in highly suggestive images of erotic temptation, the product of a garden such as has nurtured Judith's younger years. She is 'peach' and 'nectarine' and stands in direct opposition to Mabel Fuller, another first-year undergraduate who turns to Judith with something of the same adoration that Judith reserves for Jennifer.

In its analysis of the subject of women's education and the possibilities held out to women in the liberated post-war society of the 1920s, *Dusty Answer* reveals something of the uneasiness and contradictions that beset the issue. The portrait of Mabel Fuller offers an alternative picture of the educated woman, the stereotypical bluestocking that Judith fears being identified with. 'Perhaps this was what really clever girls looked like' (p. 113), she worries, as she gazes on Mabel's thick glasses and even thicker body with dread. Yet Mabel's portrayal, which is at first in danger of becoming a caricature, eventually develops into a more feeling study of a girl who is permanently ostracised through natural and social disadvantages, her personal plainness, her lower middle-class origins and her lack of social polish. To some extent, however, she also projects Lehmann's own nervousness at being thought to compromise her femininity by scholarship, and her consequent anxiety over what constitutes the modern woman. The novel is concerned to illustrate that brains and beauty are not necessarily incompatible, for Jennifer Baird is the most brilliant history student of her year and Judith too 'acquits herself with distinction' in her Tripos. In what is perhaps a betrayal of her own misgivings, Lehmann somewhat cruelly allows Mabel to fail.

Jennifer and Mabel offer antithetical models of New Womanly behaviour, models that Judith needs to negotiate before she can arrive at a knowledge of self. They are also used to investigate Judith's own subliminal lesbianism, for she is on the one hand deeply attracted to Jennifer – admiring her physical loveliness and the perfection of her nude body, and drawn in to open confessions of love – and simultaneously threatened by Mabel's equally strong attraction to her. The exploration of bisexuality, apparent in the portrayal of Judith, Jennifer and Roddy, whose real proclivities remain unclear, is a central feature of this novel. Girton in particular is evoked as a community of women where the feelings of sisterhood and feminine allegiances are allowed to expand. As an only child Judith finds that at Cambridge, for the first time, she is in a community of equals, sharing womanly confidences, jokes and an intimacy such as she has never known. It is possible to identify this sense of the importance of female bonding as a phenomenon directly related to the effects of the First World War, surfacing in a number of post-war works by women writers as different as Winifred Holtby and Radclyffe Hall. In their provocative analysis of women and modernism, Sandra Gilbert and Susan Gubar observe that

> just as important as the female eroticism that the war ener-
> gized . . . was the more diffusely sensual and emotional sense
> of sisterhood that the 'Amazonian countries' created by the
> conflict inspired in nurses and VADs, land girls and tram
> conductors, ambulance drivers and armament workers.[47]

Certainly in its Cambridge episodes *Dusty Answer* projects a vision of a female world that liberates women's emotional potential in an atmosphere where men are marginalised.

Jennifer's ultimate defection to the explicitly lesbian Geraldine Manners pursues to its conclusion the implications of the more tentative relationship she has enjoyed with Judith. Geraldine, her very name resonantly male, is 'tall, dark and splendid . . . magnificent unfeminine physical' (p. 158). Her short hair makes her 'masculine' and she 'smoked like a man' (p. 164). She engages in wrestling matches with Jennifer on the lawn (surely a more than incidental comparison with the homo-erotic wrestling scene between Rupert Birkin and Gerald Crich in Lawrence's *Women in Love*, published five years earlier), and appears to Judith 'the embodiment of all hitherto uncoordinated and formless fears, the symbol for change, and dark alarms and confusions' (p. 158). Yet while repelled by Geraldine's overt masculinity, Judith reluctantly recognises her attraction, aware that 'her person held an appalling fascination' (p. 171). This ambivalence towards lesbianism, an underlying feature in several of Rosamond Lehmann's novels, can be detected in other contemporary works by women whose sense of gender allegiance was unclear. Virginia Woolf's Mrs Dalloway feels profoundly unnerved by the unwomanly Miss Kilman while yet able to recall with tenderness her passionate arousal in the rose garden with Sally Seton. For Lehmann, as for Woolf, the power struggle that all love-affairs embody takes on a different and troubling dimension in its lesbian form, complicating the heroine's hold on her own tenuously grasped sexual identity.

In *Dusty Answer* essentialist concepts of both femininity and masculinity are challenged in this way. The androgynous Geraldine Manners functions as a complement to the equally Bohemian figure of Tony Baring who exerts such magnetism over Roddy. For just as Geraldine is a classic lesbian construction, so Tony is the effete homosexual, a poet with a voice that is 'soft and precious', a lisp and 'thin, unmasculine hands' (p. 96). He calls Roddy 'darling' and, despite his jealousy of her, Judith is powerless in the face of his implacable hold over the man they both desire. Jennifer and Roddy, both bisexual and themselves confused, feature as characters who allow Judith's own burgeoning sexuality to express itself, while Geraldine and Tony pose threats to her self-confidence, though ultimately they extend her understanding of the complexity of sexual allegiances and her own erotic nature. As one commentator has observed of novels and of artists of the period, 'to be merely of one sex was rather ungenerous'.[48] Lehmann's adventurousness in her presentation of unorthodox sexuality is concomitant with her direct investigation into the construction of personal and especially female identity. The centrality of eroticism to Judith's search for self can also be linked to some extent with the force of the Lawrentian ethic during this period as well as with the general post-war displacement of the stability of gender and gender relations.

Yet Judith is very definitely a feminine woman, insistent on maintaining her femininity in a world where the prevailing disturbance of gender roles might well unsettle it. In a culture where style tends to assume substance, she, unlike Geraldine and Jennifer, refuses to crop her hair, but keeps it defiantly long as a traditional symbol of womanhood. She enjoys being fashionably dressed and being the object of male admiration. Once she has left Cambridge, however, Judith finds that she is faced with unacceptable alternatives. The call of Bohemianism with its fashionable exoticism holds as little attraction for her as the social circuit that her mother frequents, where roles for women are dictated by hidebound convention. As Judith discovers, life with her mother involves being paraded in the role of *ingénue* in preparation for the career of professional beauty, wife and mother that it is assumed she will follow. The penultimate section of the novel, which shows the culmination of Judith's relationships with the Fyfes and her social success as a glamorous young woman in her mother's image, is also one of the most unconventional. Its compression of the three love-affairs into one short section gives a new twist to the traditional fictional denouement. In it, Lehmann has her heroine question the models that are offered her on her 'entrance into the world' and in turn reject each one. Her relationships with Roddy, Martin and Julian, each a condensed version of a familiar love-story, indicate the roles cast for her by heterosexual love. Only when she has been through this educative process, so different from the education she underwent at Cambridge, can she exorcise the ghost of the Fyfe glamour together with her own romantic illusions.

The first stage of this anti-romantic plot, the affair with Roddy, is seen as an intrinsic part of Judith's process of maturation, and its treatment in this novel is a mark of just how far Lehmann has departed from the received fictional approach to this subject. Judith's adolescent infatuation with Roddy is allowed to run its full course. Her seduction under the willow trees in the moonlight is the culmination of the desire she has harboured since childhood, but its sequel shatters her faith in romance. Her disillusionment is a natural consequence of her discovery of the reality of sexual encounters and the different significance it can acquire for men and women. To Judith physical intimacy is the seal on romance, the perfect moment of acknowledgement of mutual love and a prelude to marriage. For Roddy, the encounter under the trees is merely one in a series of pleasant experiences, an enjoyable part of flirtation, 'a light flame of passion, blown out, relit again' (p. 229), devoid of serious intent. It is this realisation that shocks Judith from her dreams into the harshness of the modern world, and Roddy's rejection of her assumptions about their future together that produce her despair, as she feels that 'the shame of her surrender, her letter, her unrequited love would go on gnawing, burning, till the end of her life' (p. 230).

In turn the three men project onto Judith their image of woman as other, an image that they have been encouraged to develop through their early association with Mariella, the Fyfe sister and cousin. For Mariella has allowed her own identity to become

compromised in the shelter of male companionship. For much of
the novel she has been a shadowy, virtually faceless character,
without definition other than her elegance, grace, breeding and
composure. She is sister, lover, wife, mother, without apparently
being touched or changed by these, to Judith, profound experiences. At the end of the novel, her pathetic letter to Julian reveals
her as still a child, barely literate, stumbling towards articulacy,
loving hopelessly and doomed to be a victim. Only in the one encounter with Judith in the river near their home, yet another
bathing scene, does she come close to showing her true feelings –
but here the moment of revelation and communion between the
women is shattered by the intrusion of a male voice invading
their female intimacy. As a literary construction, Mariella remains
undeveloped, but her presence carries a warning to Judith of the
dangers of the Fyfes and their power to strip women of their
individuality.

For Roddy, Judith is a *femme fatale*, to be taken casually and
just as casually abandoned. He cannot see beyond the gauche signals she emits to the passionate commitment she would be
prepared to make. For Martin, on the other hand, the solid representative of the English gentry, Judith represents the future of that
heritage. He can see in her, in her role of wife and mother of his
children, only the continuance of family and a way of life endemic to the English landed classes. Momentarily attracted by the
promise of security that this life holds out to her, and desolate
after her rejection by Roddy, Judith allows herself to be tempted
into an engagement, though she quickly realises her error. The
sort of safety that Martin offers is not for Lehmann heroines,
although they recognise its value. Rather they (Judith, Grace, Olivia, Sybil and Rebecca) yearn after danger and excitement,
despite the risks such relationships incorporate. Martin's traditional code places Judith firmly in an orthodox and valued
position, but it is a position that cannot satisfy her modern
consciousness.

In a similar way Julian, always the most sensual of the cousins,
offers Judith an equally traditional but more cosmopolitan role as
his mistress. He asks her to share a life of Continental decadence,
a sybaritic existence of the European *beau monde*, without the
formal ties of marriage, ties that, he argues, would only stultify

the dynamism of their relationship. When Judith realises that 'Now I have been kissed by all three of them' (p. 271), her awakening puts the final seal on her childish fantasies. Only when she has tested these fantasies against the reality that each man offers can she escape her illusions and face the future as her own person.

For in this fourth section of the novel, Judith's disaffection from the available social routes open to women is clearly demonstrated. In the world to which her mother introduces her, femininity has become a high art form. Judith, attired *à la mode*, bejewelled and graceful, has acquired the outward signs of womanliness so acceptable in chic society. 'You wear beautiful clothes. You carry yourself to perfection. You have an air', Julian tells her, 'What are you going to do with it all?' (p. 261). But Judith's mother is a role model whose aridity Judith can only reject, and it is part of Lehmann's subtlety that at the same moment as she makes Julian's proposal sound tempting, she also exposes the glittering life he offers as essentially life-denying, 'that thick, steamy world, in the mingled soils of sickly heat, bilious faces, rich food, sensual dancing, heavy scents of women, applied bow mouths, soft perspiring flesh' (p. 262).

This ambivalence is crucial to Lehmann's approach both here and in her subsequent works. All the brilliant episodes of the book, whether comic or romantic, together with the analysis of Judith's growth to self-understanding, are undercut by an awareness of tragedy that is discernible in the feverish character of post-war hedonism. Charlie's death, Julian's experience of battle, Martin's drowning, her father's death – each loss causes Judith to pause, to reassess her sense of self and her understanding of the duplicitous nature of human experience, that jagged rock concealed beneath the shimmering surface of the cool bathing-pool. It is this alternative, dark side to experience that gradually becomes the dominant tone in Lehmann's writing, from the hesitant sombreness of *A Note in Music*, through the painful dismantling of romance in *The Weather in the Streets* to the harsh, uncompromising realism of *The Echoing Grove*.

The ending of *Dusty Answer* shows Judith having lost all ties with the past. 'I am all uprooted and don't know what I shall do' she confides to Julian (p. 286), but discarding her childhood means that she is now ready for adult life. A moment of epiphany occurs when she glimpses Roddy, accompanied by Tony Baring, pass by without noticing her on a Cambridge street. 'She seemed to wake up suddenly' in her realisation that 'she had tried to make a reality out of the unreality' (p. 301). The closing paragraphs of the book carry a deliberately Chekhovian allusiveness as Judith returns home with the certain knowledge that the cherry tree, the symbol of her youthful illusions, will be cut down. That same tree has featured as a false symbol of immaculate beauty and perfection throughout the novel. 'Cherry blossom grows from the seeds of enchantment', Judith tells Martin at one point (p. 101). Echoes of the pear tree in Katherine Mansfield's 'Bliss' also permeate the image, and, as in that story, the heroine's arrival at maturity must coincide with her understanding that the enchantment is over. She must wake up to reality and the loneliness of self in a world where 'she had nobody but herself and that was best' (p. 303).

The solitude that Lehmann envisages for her heroine in the final scenes of *Dusty Answer* provides the starting-point for *A Note in Music*, a work that continues and develops many of the themes initiated in the first book. Although the mood of subdued defeatism that dominates the second novel deterred contemporary readers who had hoped for a repetition of the buoyancy of *Dusty Answer*, in formal terms the work demonstrates an advance, and provides a site from which to trace Lehmann's subsequent development. *A Note in Music* is virtually plotless, taking a year in time (from January to December) in Grace Fairfax's life and using the changing of the seasons as emotional indicators in her unspoken currents of feeling. In Lehmann's deliberate experimentation with technique, the narrative perspective is no longer confined to the consciousness of the central character but enters into the perceptions of all the characters in turn, both major and minor, a method that Lehmann was to employ with more dexterity in her next work, *Invitation to the Waltz*. Despite the often skilful observation and dramatic variety of the text, neither Tom's voice nor the voice of the working-class shopgirl, Pansy, are captured with conviction. Pushed beyond her range, Lehmann cannot here reproduce a confident male register or handle an unfamiliar social dimension with real authority.

At the centre of *A Note in Music* is a study of Grace Fairfax, a woman trapped in a stultifying marriage. Her husband, Tom, is set in his ways and in his job as office clerk in a dull industrial town, and Grace's only friend is Norah Mackay, whose husband, Gerald, is a provincial university professor. In varying degrees all four characters sense their own failure and this feeling is exacerbated by the arrival of Hugh Miller, the nephew of the owner of the firm where Tom is employed. Like the Fyfes in *Dusty Answer*, Hugh and his sister Clare represent the world of educational and social advantage, wealth, landed estates, travel and glamour, and their impact on Grace, Norah and Gerald is brief but substantial. In the central summer episode of the novel, a day spent on a country estate belonging to distant cousins of Norah helps to revivify their staid lives. Subsequently Grace goes on holiday alone to the south of England to try to recapture her sense of inner peace in preparation for a resumption of her mundane existence. The book concentrates on non-fulfilment, on characters coming to terms with their own inadequacies and their circumstances, and its mood of harsh realism contrasts sharply with the spell-binding romanticism of *Dusty Answer*. Grace's unspoken love for Hugh has, however, a transforming effect on her life, and after he has left the town she is able to reconcile herself to her marriage and her unsatisfactory husband with some equanimity.

A series of negative images in the opening chapter of the novel establishes the oppressive atmosphere of the northern provincial town as Grace dresses on a chill January evening for an undistinguished dinner at home with her husband. The woman who sits down to fish pie and chocolate shape for supper in a dingy dining-room seems to be the very antithesis of the lively and talented Judith Earle whose life was so full of promise. Yet Grace, approaching middle age, apparently incapable of self-expression, has learned to cultivate a mask of indifference and impassivity in order to hide the misery that lies beneath. 'It was the only thing left worth doing, she thought – to be like stone before the world; to tell no one "I also suffer"' (pp. 8–9).

As the narrative enters into each character's consciousness in turn, so each is revealed as acting a part, and each in some way reproduces the feeling of repression and lost potential that Grace openly acknowledges in the opening section of the book. Into this drear setting comes Hugh Miller, disrupting for a brief time the monotony of the others' lives. His disturbing presence acts as a catalyst for Grace, Norah and Gerald, his youthful vigour and dynamism reminding them of their own missed opportunities, and ultimately enabling them to come to terms with the paths they have chosen for themselves. For Grace, Hugh is the romantic realisation of fantasies she never knew she had, embodying boundless vitality and promise that bring the hopelessness of her marriage and the inconsequential routine of her days into sharp relief. Watching him out walking with his sister, Clare, she invests them with symbolic status. They become an enchanted couple, 'dreamlike images in the midst of light, echo, movement' (p. 85), making her own isolation more pronounced than before, as she instils them with 'that excess of mystery, that weight of meaning which they were to bear for her henceforth for ever after' (pp. 89–90). Hugh's presence causes Grace to reassess her life and to attempt to recapture something of her own youth.

In identifying the beginning of her lapse into inertia with the moment of leaving her father's house to get married, Grace becomes aware that

> the further she had emerged into the world from that loved shelter and protection the more her essential weakness of character, her reluctance to deal with responsibilities, her inability to cope with daily duties, had become manifest; and little by little, in her idleness and stagnation, the visual sensibility which had inspired her childhood had petered out. (p. 96)

The acuteness of Grace's childhood apprehension has been dulled in desolate conditions that have rendered it unproductive. It is a theme that Lehmann returns to in both her fictional and non-fictional works, as she examines the sources of imaginative creativity through her heroines and through her own self-analysis, attempting as a mature writer to recapture the vividness of her early impressions. The loss of inspiration that now characterises Grace Fairfax's life is introduced early in the text through references to her dead child and her inability to nurture any form of life, even the pet puppy she had adored. The links between maternal and imaginative fertility, which are indicated only provisionally in *A Note in Music*, are built up more systematically in Lehmann's later novels to provide an extensive analysis of the nature of female potential. In particular, *The Ballad and the Source* takes the image of maternal frustration as the pivot of the narrative, but it appears too in both *The Weather in the Streets* and *The Echoing Grove*, where equally graphic abortion and stillbirth sequences emphasise the psychological and cultural consequences of thwarted motherhood.

A Note in Music introduces yet another distinctive Lehmann theme, the importance of the past and its role in determining and dominating the present. For Grace, it is marriage to the wrong man that has arrested her emotional development, and it is Hugh's dynamism that alerts her to the implications of her choice. Her solitary escape to a holiday retreat (the location kept deliberately vague) puts her into 'a summer trance' (p. 190), an idyllic space that she creates apart from her normal routine. It is a space that allows for a detached appraisal of her situation and for a return to her country origins and a reliving of her childhood innocence. The regularity of her husband's weekly letter serves as a reminder of her real entrapment in a monotony from which escape is only an illusion. At the close of the summer episode she returns to the life she has chosen, but now with a greater tranquillity than before. *A Note in Music* provides the first articulation of the equivocal treatment of nostalgia that is one of the distinguishing traits of Rosamond Lehmann's fiction. In this novel, as in *Invitation to the Waltz* and *The Ballad and the Source*, the past represents a world of innocence and pleasure, but also of immobility and lack of progression. Grace Fairfax cannot remain in a permanent summer or in a state of non-responsibility, but she needs to accommodate the past before she can contemplate her future. The same is true of Norah Mackay, who embarks on a nostalgic journey during the day spent at her family's country estate. Walking again through grounds that she had known as a child, she remembers episodes from her youth and in particular dwells on memories of her first lover, a casualty of the First World War. Norah's memories are therapeutic. In reliving the past she is able to recover an inner resource that helps her to cope with the stale marriage that has become her adult life. Here, as in *Dusty Answer* and Lehmann's subsequent works, the War functions as a point of change in characters' lives, an event that fundamentally altered the directions they could take. The young girl who was Norah 'had danced with such a particular swimming grace, that she had actually thought of embarking on a professional training. The war and being a VAD had put a stop to all that' (p. 143). The War too has interfered with Gerald's professional career, ending his hopes of a fellowship at Cambridge. The embittered cynic who figures in *A Note in Music* is contrasted with the stimulating intellectual of romantic temperament he might have become. His brief romance with Hugh's sister, Clare, reanimates his confidence and, like Grace's love for Hugh, its transient nature helps him towards a new understanding and acceptance of his present circumstances.

Ironically, Hugh Miller, who is the agent of the characters' self-realisation, is perhaps the least mature of all the characters, supremely oblivious to his impact on their lives. Sealed in a life of privilege, he cannot see beyond the surface composure that the others present to the outside world, and on the one occasion when Grace's unhappiness becomes dangerously evident, he is clearly terrified of the emotional demands she might make. 'A deep antagonism filled him, a desire to fly. He simply could not help despising, recoiling from any one who wanted pity. The more he tried to force himself, the colder he felt' (p. 241). As an English upper-class male, bred in the classic aristocratic tradition, Hugh embodies the inhibitions of his culture, unable to acknowledge his sublimated homosexual leanings and refusing to admit to the reasons for his lack of response to women. He runs away from both Grace and Pansy when he suspects them of encouraging intimacies, whether emotional or sexual, just as in the past, at university, he has fled from Oliver, a character who never appears directly in the novel, but whose presence is a powerful force in the portrayal of both Hugh and of Ralph Seddon, the young Oxford aesthete. Indeed, it is through the portrait of Ralph Seddon, sensitive and self-analytical, unafraid of expressing his love for men, that Hugh's inadequacies are brought into focus. The interest in homosexuality, in the thin dividing line between friendship and passion, and in the barriers stationed between men and women, all present in *Dusty Answer*, are retained as thematic strands in this novel, and are developed with varying degrees of prominence in Lehmann's subsequent work.

A Note in Music has never been as popular with Lehmann readers as it deserves. Its low-key treatment of its subject relies on inference and understatement rather than extended analysis of narrative situations. Its fragmentary technique, each of its short sections corresponding to an emotional as well as a meteorological climate, deliberately avoids conclusiveness. It begins in January, cold, blank and hopeless, and ends with the onset of winter at the close of the same year. The pursuit of intensity that was such a feature of *Dusty Answer* stops short of realisation in *A Note in Music*, where characters' feelings are implied rather than explored in detail. Yet the novel takes the apparently blank lives of nonentities to hint at the emotional turmoil and frustrations that lie beneath the surface. 'How profoundly each individual life is concealed' (p. 161) observes Ralph Seddon, a character endowed with some insight. It is the approach formed in *A Note in Music* to the dichotomy of experience, the disparity between public mask and private turbulence that forms much of the basis for Rosamond Lehmann's subsequent fiction.

4

Growing Up:
Invitation to the Waltz

Invitation to the Waltz is a more assured and a more original composition than Rosamond Lehmann's earlier novels. It is also alone among Lehmann's fictions in being more comic than romantic in tone, its darker elements kept to the margins of the novel's mood, always present but never allowed to dominate. It is a work that makes outstanding use of minimal materials, selecting only fragments of experience from the life of a young girl over two days. Yet through this evocation of the transient moment, it manages to convey a sense of a complete society in flux. Specifically, through its focus on an isolated fragment of adolescent experience, the novel powerfully re-creates the texture of an individual life – awkward, uneasy, waiting, poised on the edge of knowledge. In addition the book produces an impression of an England caught at a particular historical moment, at the turning-point of cultural consciousness that characterised the years following the First World War. And in the implicit connection made between the gauche adolescent and the sheltered world of which she is a product, the book consummately illustrates Lehmann's ability to create substance out of the ephemeral moment.

The story, what little there is of it, concerns Olivia Curtis, the younger daughter of a respectable country family, as she prepares for her first dance at a coming-out ball at the home of some grand neighbours, Sir John and Lady Spencer. The novel's action is divided into three episodes, each of which observes and meticulously charts a stage of the almost imperceptible progress from the innocence of childhood to the half-awareness of uncomfortable adolescence. The day of Olivia's seventeenth birthday, which takes place a week before the dance, occupies the first section of the book; the hours before the dance, as Olivia and her sister, Kate, prepare themselves for the great occasion, take up the second; the dance itself and its aftermath form the final chapters. The main events consist of nothing more spectacular than the giving and receiving of birthday presents, trying on and fitting an evening dress, the casual exchange of pleasantries with neighbours and Olivia's struggling attempts at conversation with desultory young men at the Spencers' house. Yet from this slight subject matter Lehmann weaves a tale of poignant subtlety where nothing of outward significance seems to occur but where the inner life of the heroine expands to take in an adult world of knowledge that gradually impinges on her sensibilities. It also places Olivia as central character within a cultural context that all unknowingly she reveals to the reader with an accuracy of observation that provides much deeper insights than her seventeen-year-old mind can fully articulate.

In taking Olivia's seventeenth birthday as its starting-point the novel successfully communicates the feeling of alienation that characterises many of Lehmann's heroines. At seventeen, Olivia stands apart both from the world of childhood, which she has decisively left behind, and from the world of adult understanding, which she has yet to enter. During the preparations for the Spencers' dance – preparations that embrace many of the rituals that signal the emergence into young womanhood – Olivia is made sharply aware of the difference between herself and her beautiful and *soignée* elder sister, Kate, who is already at a stage of social accomplishment that Olivia envies but cannot emulate. She is also conscious of how far she has travelled from the babyish world of her younger brother, James, whose painful and obvious anxieties and whose eccentric schoolboy interests, his knitting, his poetry and his sense of humour, seem negligible, almost laughable to his sisters. As the novel progresses, this sense of alienation becomes gradually more pronounced and at times Olivia seems to take on the role of ironic commentator on the world that surrounds her. Out for her morning walk, she observes the eccentricities of the village inhabitants, all representatives of

a generation that has had its day: Major Skinner, a pathetic rem-
nant of colonial India, bereft of the status he left behind and
unable to adjust to genuine English culture; Miss Robinson,
devoting her life to the care of her aged mother and mad sister,
while trying to scrape a meagre income from dressmaking; Miss
Mivart, a gentlewoman in reduced circumstances, a reminder of
the Edwardian leisured classes whose womenfolk were not trained
to earn their own living. All are faded relics of the past, whose
lives have withered and who are forced to rely on their memories
for succour rather than on any prospect of future happiness.

It is not merely the adults, however, with whom Olivia finds
she has nothing in common. Reggie Kershaw, the hastily acquired
partner who accompanies the Curtis girls to the dance, typifies a
particular brand of English masculinity, his deliberately hearty
anti-intellectualism repellent to Olivia's finer sensibilities. Reggie,
preparing for the clergy, is committed to a simple-minded continuation of the standards of the past generation, and his crass
insensitivity is anathema to Olivia's finely tuned responses. At the
Spencers' dance, the climactic centre of the novel, Olivia can
only feel isolated from the *savoir faire* that seems to characterise
the members of the Spencer household and their friends. Her
childhood friend, Marigold, has taken off into a new world 'away
from shared classes, away from asking them to schoolroom tea,
from mutual jokes and confidences, from all the happy boredom,
the busy emptiness, the melancholy, dreaming happiness of their
common adolescence, to a world where they could not follow her'
(p. 161). And as she goes through the evening, Olivia's dancing
partners successively intensify her sense of non-belonging, their
male interests and lack of sensitivity contributing only to her feelings of inadequacy and exclusion. This sense of exclusion,
however, embodies far more than a purely personal discomfort.
Not only does Olivia acquire the representative status of all
adolescent experience but she comes to suggest a number of
social divisions: of age; of gender; of class; of intellectual from
Philistine; and of the forward-looking face of openness and
change that will signal the new twentieth century from the retro-
grade attitudes of the others.

For in opening the novel with a portrait of Olivia Curtis and
her family, Lehmann is doing far more than painting a purely

domestic picture, however well observed that picture might be. The Curtis family, with its different generations and ramifications, is a family with a strong sense of history, and the village they inhabit is a place that serves as a neat illustration of the historical processes that have made England what it is in 1920. Lehmann is careful to establish the family's descent from their mid-nineteenth-century industrialist patriarch, Olivia's great-grandfather. As the novel prepares the way for Olivia's transition from her past world of childhood into a fresh stage in her feminine career, so it places her in a cultural environment of family and local history. The Curtis household is laden with tokens of its heritage. The rooms are crowded with family photographs, 'watercolour performances of aunts and great-aunts thick upon the walls' (p. 2) and furniture that has been handed down from ancestors. The way of life that Olivia, her brother and sister are born into is one reliant upon tradition, with roast beef and apple tart on Sundays as reminders of a durability that is stable and comforting.

In the first few pages of the novel Lehmann establishes an authorial perspective from which to view the events that follow. Using an almost cinematic technique, she first creates a panoramic vista of the village of Little Compton and then places the Curtis family in its precise historical location before moving in to a narrow focus, a particular time of day and a certain individual. 'These walls enclose a world. Here is continuity spinning a web from room to room, from year to year. It is safe in this house. Here grows something energetic, concentrated, tough, serene; with its own laws and habits' (p. 4). It is as if the eye of a camera were being followed through the Curtis's gate, up the path to the front door and then to the porch and the words, 'The inner door is closed. It is winter. Quarter to nine in the morning' (p. 5). Symbolically moving through the interior door, Lehmann takes us into the consciousness of her *ingénue* heroine but makes it clear that this is a consciousness that is informed and determined by the age in which she is born. By setting Olivia against her family history and the life of the neighbourhood and against the world of advantage revealed by the Spencer household, Lehmann establishes a vivid sense of class and social divisions, and of the impact of social forces that bear down upon and determine the course of individual lives. The book also, in its delineation of the

interaction between parents and children, provides a foretaste of
the generational conflict that is always of permanent interest in
Lehmann's fiction and that plays a more decisive role in the
sequel to this novel, *The Weather in the Streets*.

Invitation to the Waltz has its source in the English fictional
tradition of the comedy of manners and domesticity that has provided a framework for English women novelists since the
eighteenth century. Indeed Rosamond Lehmann's work has been
compared with Jane Austen's for its acuity of observation, the
sure comic handling of dialogue and for its similar choice of
milieu, the English gentry at play. As with Jane Austen's novels it
is easy to dismiss Lehmann as little more than an accomplished
miniaturist, offering a slice of a life, brilliant in its comic accuracy but limited in its scope. 'As Miss Lehmann advanced in
technique, in delicacy, in assurance', wrote a contemporary reviewer of her work shortly after the publication of *Invitation to
the Waltz*, 'so she retired from life in all its larger manifestations'.[49] The comment is typical of appreciations of Rosamond
Lehmann's fiction, the praise reserved for her accomplished handling of material while damning the insubstantiality of the material
itself. This sort of approach ignores the sense of a society in transition that provides the context for the action of many of
Lehmann's works, and forms a main subject of enquiry in *Invitation to the Waltz*. For in this novel, Olivia's personal uncertainty
reflects the tensions and uncertainties of a post-war society,
recovering from the consequences of the devastating conflict of
1914–18 and in many ways resistant to the signs of change that
threaten its stability. Everywhere are indications of the effects of
the war, in the story of the blind war veteran whom Olivia meets
at the dance, the young Timmy Douglas, permanently exiled from
the life he was born to enjoy; in the mementoes of her dead son
that adorn Lady Spencer's dressing-table; and in the evidence of
the losses that the village community, with its array of spinsters,
has sustained. Even the comic dressmaker, Miss Robinson, is a
pathetic reminder of the fate of single women in a society where
the supply of eligible bachelors has been decimated. 'Where are
the young men?' asks the omniscient narrative voice of the opening pages of the novel, going on to remark in a voice
self-consciously tinged with sentimental nostalgia, 'The mould is

the same but it is cracked: the flavour is strange; it dissipates itself; it is spent' (p. 2). This is the voice that creates the framework for the book. The world that Olivia knows is one that is still nominally attached to a gracious way of living dominated by a sense of continuity and traditional values. Assumptions are made about birthday rituals, about the formal etiquette of a dance, about the proper place of servants. The novel also suggests ways in which these practices affect women's roles in their perpetuation of paternalism and the maintenance of rigid social barriers. Yet throughout the book there are signs of the imminent change that will banish these values to the sidelines and hints too that the leisured classes themselves have already become something of an anachronism. Peter Jenkins, the young misfit whom Olivia meets at the dance, might be a satiric portrait, a comic parody of a disaffected rebel, but he also voices opinions that irremediably unsettle Olivia's vision of the Spencers and the codes of conduct she is being asked to accept as fixed. To him, the regal Lady Spencer is nothing more than a 'bosomy tin-plated dowager', the young girls who seem so glamorous to Olivia merely 'well-diluted debs – guaranteed wholesome and sedative' and the magical ballroom is hung with pictures of 'horsy ancestors, ancestral horses – such an interesting study' (p. 197).

Peter sees the dance and its rituals as a museum piece, the dowagers and the old men who set the rules as fossilised, and though he is dismissed as pretentious, rude and not a little defensive, his words do illuminate a way of thinking that suggests the existence of a world outside the narrow environs of provincial Tulverton and its locality. Olivia, while temporarily comforted by the confident poise of Lady Spencer, and her easy dismissal of Peter's affectedness – for the world she so serenely inhabits is one where guests do not 'overstep the bounds of permissible eccentricity by crude anti-social displays of hostility' (p. 207) – is none the less unnerved. Peter's words have managed to dislodge her unquestioning acceptance of the standards of her parents' generation, and she cannot brush off his behaviour as lightly as they can. 'What was it then that made one feel that, with just a few more clues provided, one would get to know him, understand his language?' (p. 213) she muses at one point, disassociating herself from the boorish, unthinking jollity of Reggie Kershaw and his crowd of laughing girls. Her composure is easily restored and the charm of Rollo Spencer and his father, whom she encounters towards the end of the evening, more than compensate for Peter's crudity. But Olivia's innocence has been dislodged a little from its perch, a definitive stage in a process of enlightenment that continues after the formal closure of the book. We need to remember that the novel was written in 1932 from a position of clear-sightedness denied its fictional personalities. Lehmann's heroine, Olivia, is of the same generation as her author. Her seventeenth birthday in 1920 places her as two years younger than her creator, and as a girl whose adult life will incorporate behaviour and attitudes very different from those of her parents. It is indeed the case that subsequently we see Olivia, in *The Weather in the Streets*, transgressing conventional bounds of conduct in a way that horrifies her elders, though in this later work she is at the same time made to recognise the weight of establishment values and the power that the older generation can still exert.

Yet despite its distinct and deliberate period flavour, the novel's scope encompasses experience that also transcends the details of its historical background. Part of Lehmann's achievement in *Invitation to the Waltz* is to create a sense of detachment from the world she depicts, while simultaneously evoking it precisely – this world where Nanny waits comfortingly to mend the loose hem of an evening dress, where middle-class homes contain their own schoolrooms, and where camiknickers are considered the height of *risqué* daring. Olivia's personal anxieties have at their core a familiarity that goes beyond these specific details of etiquette to reveal the terrors of emergent adolescence that are all too uneasily recognisable. One does not have to have been born in 1903 to identify with Olivia's misplaced sympathy for the lace-seller whose tale of woe rings only half true to Olivia even at the moment of parting with her precious ten-shilling note, her birthday gift from Uncle Oswald. Nor to be familiar with the literary avant-garde of the period to appreciate her feelings of inadequacy as she is made to feel the pangs of exclusion from the inner circle of Oxford's literary élite that Peter Jenkins so pretentiously alludes to.

More importantly, as she bathes, dresses and perfumes herself for the Spencers' ball, Olivia enacts the rites of social initiation that are endemic to all social systems and have particular significance for women. For closely associated in this novel with the nervousness attendant on public appearance are the special responsibilities of gender. Olivia on the evening of the dance is no longer a child but must prepare to take her place as a woman in the sexual market-place. Indeed one of the novel's major triumphs is the suggestive quality of its sexual dimension, woven into the perception of Olivia's growing up, rarely acknowledged in an overt way, but ever present none the less, however little she herself comprehends it. It is, for instance, present in the attentions of Major Skinner whom Olivia meets on her morning walk, knowing that she can bowl him over with a girlish smile; present too in the 'long, soft stares' (p. 19) from Uncle Oswald and his unnatural interest in the contents of her diary; present in the embarrassing advances of old, paunchy Mr Verity who clutches her to him as they stumble around the dance floor; and in the humiliating indifference of Archie who forgets his engagements with her at the Spencers' ball. Olivia's emergence from the chrysalis of childhood coincides with her growing sense of a self that affects and responds to male awareness of her sexuality. In addition, the book is shot through with references to the image of self as it is perceived by others, often through a refracted perspective, that of Olivia's imagining herself as the object of others' gazes.

On her birthday morning, scrutinising herself in the bedroom mirror, Olivia hopes to find a reflection that will reassure her of the momentous identity transformation she is about to undergo, for 'Nowadays a peculiar emotion accompanied the moment of looking in the mirror: fitfully, rarely a stranger might emerge: a new self.' On this occasion, however, Olivia is disappointed: 'The image failed her, remained unequivocally familiar and utilitarian' (p. 11). In the early twentieth century, as the concept of a unified personality itself came increasingly under inspection, the mirror became a popular metaphor for the fragmentation of the contemporary psyche. In D. H. Lawrence's *Women in Love* (1924), for instance, Gerald Crich, the representative of cultural disintegration, searches in a mirror to find reassurance, looking 'closely at

his own face, at his own eyes, seeking for something'.[50]
Lehmann's novels take as a central subject the issue of identity as
a social construct, and examine with increasing ferocity the
destructive effects of role playing that the process of socialisation
incorporates. *Invitation to the Waltz* treats the issue more gently
than do some of Lehmann's later works, notably *The Weather in
the Streets* and *The Ballad and the Source*, which both expose
divisions within the personality in their portrayal of characters destroyed by social and cultural pressures. In *Invitation to the Waltz*,
Olivia is only on the brink of the discovery that will make her
into the adult we find in the sequel to this book, and she is still
at the stage when the promise of adolescence might be realised.
Her mirror image is elusive, transient, offering her a number of
versions of self appropriate to the developmental stage that she is
uncertainly negotiating.

> Well, what was it? She knew what she looked like, had for
> some years thought the reflection interesting, because it was
> her own; though disappointing, unreliable, subject twenty times
> a day to blottings out and blurrings, as if a lamp were guttering
> or extinguished: in any case irremediably imperfect. But this
> was something else. This was a mysterious face. (p. 12)

The use of the mirror image to depict the vexed concept of
identity has been used variously in literature by and about women
to project the double sense of the split female self, existing as
observer and observed, the object of the male gaze. As John Berger has argued,

> Men look at women. Women watch themselves being looked at.
> Women constantly need glances which act like mirrors, remind-
> ing them of how they look, or how they should look. Behind
> every glance is a judgement. Sometimes the glance they meet
> is their own, reflected back from a real mirror. A woman is al-
> ways accompanied – except when quite alone, and, perhaps,
> even then – by her own image of herself. . . . From earliest
> childhood she is taught and persuaded to survey herself contin-
> ually. She has to survey everything she is and everything she
> does because how she appears to others, and particularly how

she appears to men, is of crucial importance for what is normally thought of as the success of her life.[51]

The concept of voyeurism as an inevitable accompaniment to female behaviour is an integral part of Rosamond Lehmann's presentation of women. References to covert as well as acknowledged observers of her heroines' performance litter her novels, whether it be Roddy's secret watch over Judith Earle's midnight swim in *Dusty Answer* or Rollo's openly lustful glances at Olivia's sylph-like form in *The Weather in the Streets.* In a number of Lehmann's novels, the mirror becomes a substitute for this male gaze, as women successively create themselves in the image they are trained to believe will evoke admiration and approval of their value as sexual merchandise. The mirror too can be used, as it is in *The Ballad and the Source,* to suggest the ultimate sterility of this fetishistic approach. In that novel, Ianthe's individual identity is crushed beneath the pressure of measuring up to imposed images, the room full of mirrors that she metaphorically inhabits resulting in a broken and a desolate life.

From Tennyson's Lady of Shalott, whose frustrated eroticism finds its complement in the mirror's second-hand pictures of romance, to Sylvia Plath's calculated 'Mirror', whose dispassionate voice objectifies female ageing and the withering of passion, the mirror has become a literary device with a history of multiple sexual inferences that relate to women's ability to develop freely. In *Invitation to the Waltz* Olivia's image is continually measured against available models of femininity and clichéd views of adolescence, which she both conforms to and subverts. She is aware of herself as a work of art, 'the portrait of a young girl in pink' (p. 11), recognising through her reflection elements of an erotic energy that she cannot otherwise express. As she moves through a 'silent, darkened house' on a summer's day, 'melancholy, solitary, restless, keyed up expectantly – for what? waiting – for whom?', Olivia's image undergoes a transition from darkness to brilliance, from restlessness to completion: 'Her body seemed to assemble itself harmoniously within it, to become centralized, to expand, both static and fluid; alive' (p. 12). As critics have noted, the very act of gazing in a mirror is for women a highly complex procedure. As she looks for something that she frequently cannot define, the woman engages in a process of self-objectification, measuring her reflected appearance against an unspecified ideal of femininity. She is in fact

> drawn into the beauty system by the force of her entire culture, by the design of the overall relationship between the sexes. When she looks into the mirror and sees ugliness reflected back upon herself, what she is actually experiencing is the value that her society has placed upon her category, that she has no value.[52]

So, when in the dressmaker's front room, Olivia turns from the magazine reproductions of modish designs to her own ungainly image in the mirror, she becomes only too aware of how far her body departs from the stylishness suggested by *Fashions For All*. Uncertainly gazing at herself, at 'the pair of knobs at the base of her neck, and the protuberant ridge of her collar-bone' (p. 50), she can see direct evidence of her failure to conform to the standards of feminine beauty promoted by the commercial images. This feeling of inadequacy is again conveyed in Lehmann's description of the sisters as, with a mixture of ceremony and excitement, they get ready for the Spencers' dance. Olivia's ideas of loveliness, formed by the models in the fashion papers, are fully realised in her vision of Kate, who, dressed for the ball, looks to Olivia 'like the girl on the cover of a Special Spring Number' (p. 133). Indeed, Kate has taken her inspiration for her appearance straight from a current number of *Vogue*. Olivia, on the other hand, cannot find any comparable model for her own appearance. Even after she has recovered from the shock of having first put on her dress back to front, she can only sense the failure of the advertised products to transform her into the glamorous heroine of her romantic imagination. For her, concepts of womanly identity are also substantially determined by her reading of cheap fiction, such as the *Daily Mirror* serials, and she can only estimate her own effectiveness according to their criteria. Her attempts to find appropriations for her self-image are consequently humorously reliant on romantic cliché. As she and Kate stand side by side looking in the mirror, Olivia mutates their reflections into pure literary slush: 'the younger girl, with her gypsy colouring, afforded a rich foil to her sister's fair beauty' (p. 134). It is her only escape route from the dismal reality that confronts her in the form of her own reflected image.

Invitation to the Waltz makes it clear that for a woman the always problematic notion of personal identity is complicated by the emphasis on the outward signs of femininity that culture incorporates. Olivia's adolescence, as it is depicted here, amalgamates the physiological changes taking place, which mark the body's move from gaucherie to grace, with the behavioural codes that insist on hair, dress, perfume conforming to preset standards that will identify her as an available sexual commodity. Yet for Olivia, these rituals of self-preparation are unnatural, 'like a lesson learned by heart, but not properly understood' (p. 126). Her age, seventeen, places her in that anomalous grey area between childhood and adulthood, an area where her personality is seen as embryonic, tentatively blossoming but still unsure of its ultimate direction. Her intellect and educational promise (she is preparing for her entrance examinations to Oxford) mark her as different from the other young girls in the village, from Marigold Spencer or from Kate, girls whose only object in life is sexual conquest and marriage. But Olivia's distinctive talents can only suggest her full potential as an individual. In the closed world of the novel's location, she is confined to her stereotypic role as 'woman'. The narcissism of Olivia's stance throughout the book – her awareness of herself as an object to be looked at, her insistence on versions of her own appearance – connects too with the portrayal of the self as literary persona. Significantly one of Olivia's birthday presents is a diary, the archetypal gift for a young girl who projects herself into a series of literary poses in order to identify her place in the world she is discovering. Diary-writing is the written equivalent of mirror-gazing, another ingredient in the process of self-visualisation. Lehmann's reproduction of Olivia's first diary entry is a brilliantly comic *tour de force*, a mocking parody of adolescent gravity that also conveys the attempts to clutch at genuine feeling and express it adequately. As Olivia moves from the tone of moral self-reproof of the traditional Puritan diary to a despairing assessment of her sentimental nature and then to romantic fantasising about the unknown Reginald Kershaw, she reveals some of the literary influences that have helped to muddy her grasp on her own identity.

But Olivia is also an aspiring artist, a story-teller whose diary functions as only one of the types of narrative she is engaged in constructing. Her romantic imagination differs from those of her predecessors, Judith Earle and Grace Fairfax, in that it becomes a conscious tool in her interpretation and evaluation of experience. Olivia's gift for imaginative fabrication makes her the first of Lehmann's heroines who are also story-tellers, a precursor of Rebecca Landon in *The Ballad and the Source*. The conflation between Olivia's consciousness and the authorial perspective dramatises characters and situations in language that imperceptibly merges the two positions. 'Some day I'll write a story about it' (p. 128), muses Olivia, casting her mind back to a scene of humiliation at a children's party years before. Her instinctive ability to fashion both herself and others into artistic products is applied to the most unlikely objects. Reggie Kershaw, the boorish partner invited to accompany the Curtis girls to the dance, becomes transformed into a self-denying committed missionary once Olivia hears that he is reading for the ministry.

> He was avoiding temptation. Neither Kate's eye, the clear, proud, challenging eye of a beauty, nor Olivia's, melting and sympathetic, should swerve him from godly thoughts, from his decision to take Holy Orders. Now they saw why he was moderate in his dancing: detached from worldly pleasures, yet in his tolerance not altogether spurning them, he would be with but not of the revellers. (pp. 146–7)

Olivia's language reveals its debt to its literary sources, the popular fiction that feeds her imagination. Advertisements, novelettes, heroic and sentimental literature all have their impact on her attempt to familiarise situations. Even Mr Verity's pathetic attempts to inspire her sympathy can be partially accommodated when she thinks that 'he must have had a Great Sorrow' (p. 232). While Olivia is used by Lehmann to help parody clichéd formulae, her very awkwardness also suggests the problems of finding appropriate expression for genuine states of feeling. Olivia is as yet unformed, not as adept as her creator in articulating the distinction between true and false emotion. The limits on her understanding are paralleled by the limits on her powers of verbalisation, and her expanding consciousness is only cautiously matched by analagous linguistic accuracy. Yet Olivia watches and assesses her own behaviour, each encounter an initiation into a new set of behavioural and linguistic codes. 'Coats were pink, dogs were hounds' (p. 210), she remembers belatedly after having a made a humiliating *faux pas* in a conversation about hunting. Each of her meetings during the day and each of her partners at the dance finds her a bemused but fascinated spectator, forced ultimately to conclude that 'Men are much, much queerer than I imagined.'

Unlike Judith Earle, Olivia is never self-pitying. Indeed, throughout the novel her portrayal is characterised by this combination of imaginative sympathy and comic exposure. Olivia is a character with whose anguish we identify and whose nervousness we take seriously. Yet she is at the same time the object of ironic amusement. As with other Lehmann heroines, Olivia's outstanding quality is her inextinguishable belief in the value of life itself, her enthusiastic response to minute sensation that shows her to be warm, sensitive and full of humanity. The scene where she unwraps her birthday presents – the bolt of flame-coloured silk, the diary, the ugly china ornament from James – offers a dramatic tableau that serves to represent her entire approach to experience. For Olivia, all sensation is offered as a breathless process of unwrapping and discovery, an eagerness to know what secret lies beneath the blank, mysterious looking surface, and a certainty that everything is potentially exciting even if she has sufficient self-knowledge to realise that disappointment is also inevitable. Her errors are understandable and immediately forgivable. As with her pretence at rapture over the china gift from James, so Olivia must dissemble in her civility to those she meets during the day ahead – to eccentric Uncle Oswald, to fumbling Major Skinner, to the witch-like Mrs Robinson.

But Olivia's unnaturally heightened response to the mundane features of village life on a dreary November afternoon is also placed in an ironic perspective. The gravity of her individual sensibility is not allowed to dominate the novel's mood but is rather tolerated as a fundamental aspect of youthful intensity.

Even Olivia herself is aware of the dangers of imaginative excess. On her morning walk, after her meeting with Major Skinner, she thinks ahead to lunch, catching herself worrying about the fate of the cabbages to be eaten, 'for it was no good brooding over the sufferings, the unjust fate of vegetables'. Indeed one-third of the way through the book, Olivia says to herself, 'It's been a full morning', after occurrences that might in another context seem to be only dull and uninspiring. While reliant on the represented perception of her central character to provide the subject and direction for the text, Lehmann's standpoint appears to recognise the dangers of immersion in an individual stream of consciousness. As a contemporary reviewer had earlier remarked of Dorothy Richardson's *Pilgrimage*, in one sense a forerunner of *Invitation to the Waltz*, 'the bleak truth is that Miss Richardson has perfected a way of saying things without having anything to say'.[53] Attuned to the pitfalls of the narrowness implicit in adherence to a single perspective, Lehmann consequently provides continuous shifts in narrative position. The dramatic interplay of the range of voices in her work both validates and undermines the importance of the individual response. So the adolescent Olivia, sensitive and enthusiastic, is placed at the centre of the novel's sympathy and the adult world is in part revised according to her fresh perceptions. At the same time her inexperience is treated with humour and the limits on her understanding are made apparent, for the book is to a large extent concerned with the imminent death of innocence, an experience that awaits Olivia but which is placed just beyond the confines of the story itself. Olivia's personal innocence functions as a parallel to the innocence of her society, a society where those in power can, for the time being, afford to ignore the uncomfortable realities that impinge on their consciousness.

The potential threat to the social superstructure finds its complement in the hints of the raw sexuality that lurks behind the romanticism of Olivia's illusions. The Spencers' household on the evening of Marigold's coming-out party might look like a fairy palace, and Marigold, in her ethereal ballgown, might resemble a virginal princess, but the house contains dark bedrooms where furtive encounters can and do take place out of sight of the brilliantly lit ballroom. The drunken talk of the elegant, aristocratic young men is full of crude innuendo, and Marigold is capable of both casual callousness towards her erstwhile lover, Timmy Douglas, and of illicit fumblings with a casual admirer in one of those bedrooms. Olivia, although she does not fully understand the implications, has already become an object of prurient interest. Uncle Oswald's abnormal curiosity in the contents of her diary is loaded with lecherous intent, so that Olivia visualises, 'that key dangling upon his paunch, at the disposal of those plump secretive paws, those pages naked at night beneath the opaque scrutiny of those caramel eyes' (pp. 28–9). To the elderly men whom she meets during the action of the novel, she is the prototype virgin, hovering on the brink of sexual discovery, and consequently food for their fantasies of seduction. Her innocence does not attract the callow young men at the ball, who prefer the more worldly Marigold Spencer or Olivia's sophisticated cousin, Etty, but Olivia is at the mercy of Major Skinner's uncomfortable appraisal, and becomes the inescapable victim of Mr Verity, whom she notices at the ball, 'dancing with the youngest girls in the room one after the other; the girls drooping a little, pressed to his paunch' (p. 230), a fate that is inevitably hers.

The sexual undercurrent that runs throughout the novel hints at the unglamorous reality that is the counterpart to Olivia's dreams of romance and perfection. For the Spencers' ball does not prove to be the sparkling event she had imagined, but is composed rather of a number of prosaic experiences that contain unpleasant truths. At the novel's core is the same theme of romantic disillusionment that provided the basis for Lehmann's first two novels. Both Archie, Olivia's childhood hero, and Etty, her ideal of style and charm, prove themselves false; Archie's snubbing indifference just as hurtful as Etty's disparagement, as Olivia notices her 'uttering some cold, some casual, uncaring betrayal' (p. 225) to an admirer at Olivia's expense. Beneath the twinkling lights of the enchanted ballroom lie lust, drunkenness, neglect and treachery. Yet none of these evils is spelt out in detail, for the central method of the text, as in *A Note in Music*, relies on inference. The story of Timmy Douglas's blindness and his consequent abandonment by Marigold must be pieced together from fragments, the significance of which escapes Olivia, but is apparent to the more knowing reader. Similarly the adulterous liaison between Marigold and Timmy is only implied, not dwelt on at length. The casual promiscuity of Etty and her circle of London friends is an illustration of their empty, pleasure-seeking lifestyle, a glimpse of which should stand as a warning to Olivia, who finds herself on the fringe of its easy charm in *The Weather in the Streets*.

Ultimately the novel as it stands offers no explicit challenge to the prevailing superstructure. There is no direct attack on the power of those in positions of authority or on the effects of social injustice, as we find in Lehmann's later work. Olivia's final conversation with Rollo Spencer and his father, towards the end of her evening at the ball, helps to confirm her romantic notions about the gentility of the English aristocracy. 'This, that she felt stood between them, was the reality about the house: kindness, tolerance, courtesy, family pride and affection' (p. 280), she thinks as she listens to their conversation. Their politeness vindicates the evening for Olivia, and cancels out in her mind the hours of embarrassment and feelings of neglect she has suffered earlier. But how genuine is the Spencers' interest in Olivia, and how far is their charm merely superficial, an acquired legacy of their breeding as English gentlemen? For Rollo's return to the beautiful Nicola Maude is inevitable and unquestioned by Olivia, and it costs Sir John very little to enquire politely after the well-being of Olivia's father. It is left to that more savage novel, *The Weather in the Streets*, to expose the unscrupulousness with which the Spencers exploit their privileged position. *Invitation to the Waltz* is content not to disturb the smooth surface with anything harsh, but throughout the novel Lehmann hints at the dark areas that are as yet beyond Olivia's understanding but nevertheless pose a threat to the stability and complacency of her world.

5

The Torment of Loving:
The Weather in the Streets

Rosamond Lehmann's mature fiction continues to explore a number of the subjects found in her earlier works: the emotional range and intensity of women's responses, the power of the past and its hold over the present, the nature of social processes, the relationship between gender and identity. The tone of her later writing, however, undergoes a significant alteration as the tentativeness that characterised *Dusty Answer* and *A Note in Music* and the gentle comedy that set the pace for *Invitation to the Waltz* are replaced by a greater seriousness and emotional depth. Together with a more cynical edge to the satire, these qualities extend the reach of the three major novels (*The Weather in the Streets*, 1936; *The Ballad and the Source*, 1944; *The Echoing Grove*, 1953) that follow *Invitation to the Waltz* and serve to communicate a sense of the immense complexity of social and personal experience with which their characters must contend. Lehmann's focus remains the inner lives of her heroines, often tremulous, always capable of intense feeling, but the scope of her work is enlarged as she examines the power structures that make up modern society, the tension between established authority and innovation, and the struggle for personal survival in a hostile environment. Olivia in *The Weather in the Streets* is not merely a young woman in the throes of a torrid affair but a confused representative of her generation of liberated and educated women whose new-found freedom has failed them. Similarly Dinah, Madeleine and Rickie in *The Echoing Grove* move beyond the confines of their own tangled relationship to show the pervasive and destructive tension between compulsive passions and constrictive social pressures. These two books, written nearly twenty years apart, show as well Lehmann's awareness of the changing nature of twentieth-century social mores, which make individuals more self-aware and more demanding, but which beneath the surface atmosphere of increased tolerance are as rigid and as punishing as ever in their crushing denial of personal opportunities.

The Weather in the Streets takes up the story of Olivia Curtis ten years after the close of *Invitation to the Waltz*. Although in one sense a sequel to the earlier book, using many of the same characters and developing several of its themes, the later novel functions quite independently of its prelude and is in many ways a more substantial work. For while it does to some extent explore the meaning of the promise that Olivia Curtis at the age of seventeen could only guess at, it does so with a bitter irony that undermines the status of the subjects which seemed so important to the adolescent protagonist of *Invitation to the Waltz*. It is in *The Weather in the Streets* that Rosamond Lehmann finds her most complete expression of the idea first broached by Judith Earle in *Dusty Answer*, the 'torment of loving', that double-edged assault on the female sensibility that ultimately affects all Lehmann's heroines. For this work is primarily a love-story and Lehmann uses this familiar format so that it functions as a reassessment of traditional narrative formulae as they apply to women, exposing romance as a protracted form of anguish rather than as a source of fulfilment. In its analysis of the relationship between Olivia and Rollo Spencer, *The Weather in the Streets* depicts the suffering that is seen to be the inevitable accompaniment to romantic love and shows how twentieth-century women, despite their veneer of emancipation, are still victims of a cultural heritage that is powerfully weighted against them. The book's sexual politics are far more overt than in Lehmann's earlier works and the text comprises a savage attack on the patriarchal establishment, complacent and hierarchical, that conspires against vulnerable women.

The story opens with Olivia, now twenty-seven, separated from her husband, Ivor, and sharing a house in London with her cousin Etty, who appeared briefly as a gay flapper in *Invitation to the Waltz*. As she travels home to visit her family in the village of

Little Compton, where her father is seriously ill, Olivia meets Rollo Spencer, the son of the Curtis's grand neighbours, the man who had enthralled her romantic imagination ten years before. He is now married to Nicola, the society beauty glimpsed only at a distance in *Invitation to the Waltz*, but, despite his married state, Olivia finds Rollo as glamorous and as seductive as ever, and soon a clandestine love-affair develops between the couple. They meet secretly in London, take occasional weekends together and manage one snatched holiday in Europe. When she becomes pregnant, Olivia is forced to seek an abortion, an episode that Lehmann describes with all its attendant horrors, and it is this experience, together with the discovery that Rollo's wife is expecting a longed-for baby, that determines Olivia to end the affair. In the closing chapters of the book, Rollo is injured in a motoring accident as he returns home from an unsatisfactory weekend with Olivia. While he is recuperating from his injuries, Olivia visits him in order to finish this episode of her life once and for all. The last scene of the novel ends on a note of ironic ambivalence as Olivia finds herself once more subject to the irresistible force of Rollo's charm and his bland assumption that their liaison will continue as before.

The bulk of the novel, however, concerns not these outward events, but the emotional and psychological action that accompanies them. As the love-affair takes its course, Olivia discovers that the initial unalloyed delight of romantic love gradually splinters as she finds herself coming under increasingly complex social pressures. The effect of her intrigue with Rollo is to isolate her from her family, to make her *persona non grata* with the Spencers, whom she has always admired, and, as she is drawn further into secrecy and deception, to distort her capacity for natural relationships in other areas of her life. The analysis of Olivia's responses to these experiences makes *The Weather in the Streets* a compelling psychological novel with a heroine torn between conflicting impulses that she does not always fully understand. The split narrative, which moves between third- and first-person narration, helps to reflect these dual aspects of Olivia's identity – the social persona and the private individual – and in depicting the tension that exists between them, the novel implicitly affirms the existence of the double life that underpins the social fiction that men and women promote as their public selves. It is this same technique that provides the inspiration for *The Echoing Grove*, where the narrative perception of each main character forms the basis for each of its separate sections, producing a complicated interplay of perspectives. In that novel, the shift of consciousness between the three central participants is used as a psychological tool, to reveal the latent neuroses that determine the subtleties of personal relationships. As the same events are replayed from different positions, so the subjective and relative nature of interpretative response is exposed. In *The Weather in the Streets*, however, the narrative interest remains firmly located in Olivia's experience, and the unsettling effect of the shifting viewpoints is reinforced by the complementary evocation of two lifestyles which are offset against one another throughout the novel. The establishment setting, which is used for the affair with Rollo and the scenes with Olivia's family, is placed in the context of, and diminished by, the alternative set of values held by the Bohemian, artistic milieu of Olivia's London friends. This world of the intellectual avant-garde is merely hinted at in *Invitation to the Waltz*, where it appears as a slightly ridiculous and unnecessary interruption into patrician society. In *The Weather in the Streets*, however, while still at times the butt of satiric exposure, it is also perceived as a genuine means of escape from the restrictive practices and set codes of the ruling class.

The Weather in the Streets has probably become the best known among Rosamond Lehmann's works since their recent revival and publication for a new generation of readers. A dramatised version of the book was shown on British television in 1984 and its title appears as a set text on a number of women's studies courses in colleges, universities and polytechnics. It is a work that seems to speak as directly to its audience of women of the 1990s as it did to their grandmothers, and this could in part be a result of its dynamic combination of traditional and radical elements. For while on one level it can be seen as a story of a fatal attraction between two people, themselves approximating to the formulaic figures of romance – the wealthy, powerful, experienced male and the impoverished, highly sensitive younger female – it also functions as a subversive work, undermining the very genre it employs so competently. For *The Weather in the Streets* skilfully exploits the conventions of romantic fiction to provide an alternative reading of that most accessible of literary forms.

In her study of romantic fiction and its audience, *Reading the Romance*, Janice Radway has argued that romance reading operates as a collective female experience, providing women with a communal identity, as their personal and emotional value-systems, so often denigrated in 'real life', are validated by the successful romance plots of popular novels. 'Romance reading and writing', she suggests, can be seen

> as a collectively elaborated female ritual through which women explore the consequences of their common social condition as the appendages of men and attempt to imagine a more perfect state where all the needs they so intensely feel and accept as given would be adequately addressed.[54]

It is the influence of romance as it operates on women within our culture that forms one of Lehmann's main subjects of enquiry in *The Weather in the Streets*. In many respects the novel celebrates the same values promoted by conventional romantic fiction: the recognition and reassurance given to women through being found sexually desirable; the satisfaction to be found in the escape into fantasy which can transform daily mundanity; the release of emotions, such as tenderness, untapped by other social experience; the mutual sympathy of a couple, miserable in their public lives, who find in their private love a source of self-confidence that is denied them elsewhere. But the novel goes far beyond an unquestioning replication of these features. By dramatising the disintegration of this fantasy at the same time as it argues for its power, the book extends the range of the romance genre, implicating its women readers in a shared experience of disillusionment while maintaining its imaginative appeal.

For undoubtedly that traditional appeal remains. The first section of the book seduces its readers into a fiction of romantic pleasure, fuelled partly by the very familiarity of its format. Olivia meets Rollo, the hero of her girlish admiration, with a shock of recognition, on a train journey that tellingly carries her back to the world of her childhood roots. Waiting anxiously for his telephone call, she is transported back in time to the period of her adolescence, her feminist leanings vanishing in the thrill of desirability. Under Rollo's gaze she becomes a young girl again, virginal and innocent, waiting for the kiss that will change her life. This is in spite of the facts: that she is a twenty-seven-year-old *divorcée* and an independent career woman, with a large circle of artistic, 'modern' friends. Yet at the end of the first section of the book, Olivia feels that her dream of perfect romance has at last materialised. 'Is it true? can it be true?' (p. 140), she asks herself in wonderment, after that first kiss in the moonlit garden. Her excitement is heightened by the need for secrecy, energising that private and elusive area of her life that has for so long lain dormant. At first the secret is to be treasured; it is only later that concealment becomes a burden. But from the beginning Olivia is forced to recognise that her identity is split between her public and private selves. 'Tomorrow I shall have grown a more solid mask', she reflects, as she accustoms herself to the idea of having a secret lover (p. 142). The distinction made between these separate aspects of the self is linked to Olivia's discovery of her own sexual nature and the erotic dimension of experience. References to the sleeping beauty motif endorse this. 'You were like a statue', Rollo tells her. 'I thought I'd never be able to bring you to life' (p. 156). It is one of the ironies of the novel that such invigorating passion is generated by a man who in many respects represents the stupefying and stultified world of the past, the world from which Olivia wishes to disengage herself. But it is a mark of Olivia's own ambivalent position that despite her leanings towards the unconventional, she remains a traditionalist at heart, 'wanting to make something important enough to be for ever' (p. 44). This fantasy of everlasting happiness is at the root of the appeal of romance, and it is a fantasy examined and ultimately discarded by Lehmann in this novel.

The shift from the third- into the first-person narrative in the second section of the novel brings us deeper into Olivia's consciousness and into a world where emotional experience dominates. *The Weather in the Streets* is much concerned with the topic of outer and inner realities, with the passage of time and its effect on individuals, and with the larger movements of history. This second portion of the book, devoted to the period when the love-affair is at its height, presents us initially with a timeless world, a world where the boundaries of objective reality seem to exist elsewhere. This is in marked contrast to the sharply defined historical perspective of Part One when discrete stages of experience are clearly distinguished and characters are placed firmly in relation to their past. In Part Two, filtered through Olivia's subjective experience, logical sequence has been abandoned, to be replaced by the rapturous moments of lovers' meetings, each occasion 'different, existing without relation to before and after; all the times were one and the same' (p. 145). The phrase used for the title of the novel, 'the weather in the streets', refers to what occurs outside the enchanted framework of this personal relationship, 'beyond the glass casing I was in', as Olivia describes it (p. 145). The image, with its associations of <u>Snow White's</u> spellbound catalepsy and of trapped, fixed, showcase objects, is deliberately ambiguous. Olivia is in a vacuum, dreamlike until her inner being is revitalised. On the periphery of her consciousness swirls a London that is comparable to T. S. Eliot's powerful evocation of urban paralysis, the 'unreal city' of the contemporary wasteland. The novel's locations are invested with a metaphorical resonance that highlights the divisions around which the text is structured, and the lovers always meet indoors, cut off from the strident bustle that surrounds them, creating a personal space and keeping at bay the inexorable force of regulated social time.

It is possible to read the romantic format of the novel as an ironic comment on the male literary establishment, which for so many years promulgated the myth of perfect love and the idealisation of the family. Inverting the courtly love tradition of the past, which conventionally focused on a youthful hero's longing for a married woman, Lehmann places an adulterous woman, no longer in her first youth, at the centre of her tale. Olivia is a woman pursued by a married man, who, although sexually attainable, remains socially elusive, the irretrievable property of another. The harsh reality of her story deflates any remnants of the idealised fulfilment that the romantic myth promises, and it is significant that after they have become lovers, it is Rollo not Olivia who insists on perpetuating the fiction of the all-conquering nature of true love. In his attitude to Olivia, Rollo's language and

behaviour are heavily redolent of romantic cliché long after
Olivia has realised the hollowness of the paraphernalia of courtship. He sends her flowers, buys her jewellery and throughout
their affair continues to call her 'darling' rather than use her
name, effectively diminishing her status to that of his mistress
rather than recognising her as a separate person. His actions
illustrate his trust in the palliative function of love, an attempt to
console an abused woman by convincing her that her marginalised role is central.

For, as recent critics have pointed out, the romance ideology is
frequently merely a mask for a study of economic relations.[55] In
a love-story with a happy ending, women gain social ascendancy
through male wealth and status. It is only by marrying the man
who courts them that they can align their erotic desires with the
need for economic security and thus achieve a goal that their
cultural codes have decreed as acceptable. *The Weather in the
Streets* shows the opposite side of this coin through the depiction
of a woman who discovers that illicit passion fails her on both
emotional and economic grounds. As their charmed circle gradually disintegrates, the story of Olivia and Rollo's love-affair
becomes revealed as a story of male power and female helpless-
ness. 'It's a very sad thing how much men make women cry' (p.
76), Rollo observes lightly at the very beginning of the book, in
ironic anticipation of their future relationship. And as Olivia subsequently realises, 'You don't like women really do you?' (p.
161). It is typical of Rosamond Lehmann's heroines that they fall
for unsuitable men. As Rebecca Landon in *A Sea-Grape Tree* ac-
curately observes, speaking for them all, 'I like unpleasant
characters.' 'I believe you do', replies her lover. 'I'm afraid you
do. Something tells me that's your trouble' (*A Sea-Grape Tree*, p.
75). Olivia, Rebecca, Judith, Dinah and even Sybil Jardine are
natural victims who court danger in their search for passionate
experience. Rebecca articulates the urgency they all share when
she declares that 'I *cannot* live without love' (ibid., p. 26). Although the greatest fear of these women is that of being unloved,
the love they seek must be accompanied by an element of danger.
The comfortable devotion, such as Martin offers Judith in *Dusty
Answer* or Tom unthinkingly gives Grace in *A Note in Music*, cannot satisfy these passionate individuals who invite suffering and

abuse in their pursuit of romantic fulfilment. In *The Weather in the Streets*, it becomes evident that Rollo, the representative of patriarchal attitudes, sees women as possessions, to be bought, arrayed, displayed and enjoyed, but definitely relegated to the ranks of second-class citizens. As Olivia astutely remarks about his choice of restaurants, the scenes of so many of their assignations, Rollo would 'never eat anywhere inferior or female' (p. 162). Despite Olivia's resistance to being categorised as a 'kept woman', she cannot prevent others classifying her in this way. And without the public support of her lover, her experience becomes fragmented and her identity consequently nullified.

In this, as in other aspects of the treatment of this age-old motif, the love-story, *The Weather in the Streets* is a very modern text. In its exposure of the myth of romance it also examines the implications of passionate experience for a twentieth-century sexually liberated woman who is yet enmeshed by the conditions of her erotic nature. Although its central subject of a love-affair might seem at first glance conventional, *The Weather in the Streets* is highly unorthodox in its approach to this theme. In taking the figure of 'the other woman' as its heroine, and treating her plight with sympathy, it offers an unusual perspective on a familiar situation – a perspective that shocked its contemporary audience. Olivia Curtis is no Emma Bovary, naïvely embarking on an affair with a misguided notion of her own responsibilities. Nor does she engage in a casual flirtation in order to stave off boredom. She is an educated woman of the post-war generation whose emotional and sexual demands form a vital component in her total personality. In addition she has a marked degree of self-knowledge and a formed intelligence, capable of making astute judgements on the society around her. Indeed, much of the novel, filtered through Olivia's perception, consists of a satiric portrait of the aristocratic high life and the fashionable intelligentsia of the 1930s. Olivia is in fact the consummate Lehmann heroine, combining both passion and intelligence, qualities explored in equal measure in the text.

By investigating the significance of passion for a contemporary woman, Lehmann probes both the nature of female sexuality and the social constructions of femininity. The female characters in *The Weather in the Streets* are defined by those around them in terms of their social roles. Olivia is aware when she returns to Little Compton of just how anomalous a figure she is. Neither married nor single she creates difficulties for her family and their neighbours by her refusal to fit easily into a conventional category.

Similarly Etty, welcomed ten years before as a Bright Young Thing of the 1920s, is now only just tolerated by the Curtises. She has become a pathetic figure, a single woman desperately trying to retain the impression of carefree youth in a life that is essentially devoid of purpose now that her chances of finding a husband seem uncertain. Olivia's sister, Kate, on the other hand, is protected from any breath of disapproval by the sanctuary of marriage, having brought satisfaction to her parents by realising their ambitions for their daughter's future. The analysis of the success or failure of characters to live up to expectations is an important feature of a text that is deeply critical of ways in which gender roles are interpreted and judged by contemporary standards. The abortion episode that occupies Part Three of the book does not merely evoke the personal torture of such an experience but has a marked political point. The abortionist is a dealer in women, professionally exploiting their physiology and using their money to purchase expensively crafted statuettes of female nudes. The bronze models in his office that he fingers lasciviously 'with his notable white hands' (p. 289) make it clear that to him the female body is nothing more than object, whether a source of income or a collector's item.

Paradoxically the social context that facilitates such degradation also elevates motherhood, within marriage, to a sacrosanct level. The Spencers' cousin, Mary, assumes that maternity carries with it a cachet of moral superiority. Olivia's sister, Kate, and Rollo's wife, Nicola, from the safety of their married state, can luxuriate in motherhood and pregnancy respectively, and be celebrated for fulfilling a natural function. Olivia, on the other hand, must abort the foetus she has conceived from extramarital passion, knowing that, as an unmarried mother, society will offer her no protection. The episode provides an explicit illustration of the oppositional roles of men and women in contemporary society. Discovering her pregnancy, Olivia sees herself as 'the female, her body used, made fertile, turning resentful, in hostile untouchability from the male, the enemy victorious and malignant' (p. 230). She discovers too a chain of women who have shared her plight, starting with Etty, whose way of life once seemed so glamorous to her naïve country cousins. Shameful, unwanted pregnancy is a condition that unites women in a submerged network of communication, a condition unspoken and concealed from the superstructure of polite social relations. The agonising consequences of illicit love are visualised again in *The Echoing Grove*, where the scene of Dinah's stillbirth delivery once more presents women as isolated and in pain, risking death in the punishing aftermath of passion. Both *The Weather in the Streets* and *The Echoing Grove* show women as victims, seduced into relationships that are by their very nature divisive. In these texts love offers no warm embrace of sensuous gratification or comfort, but forms a process of slow and inexorable torment, socially and emotionally isolating, the physical suffering acting as an objective correlative for the emotional agony that it accompanies. •

In its searching examination of women's vulnerability, *The Weather in the Streets* also investigates the social determinants of gender. From the very beginning of the novel, suggestions are made that question the whole concept of established gender identity. At home with her family Olivia behaves in a way of which her more conventional sister disapproves. She uses language that is considered improper for a woman, dresses carelessly, laughs in an unladylike manner. The only occasion on which she meets with unqualified approval is when she is dressed to go out to dinner, wearing clothes borrowed from Kate, transformed into an immaculate copy of femininity, but sensible that she only mimics the poise and grace of a traditional model of female perfection. Despite her age, the mirror shows her 'a young girl, and a pretty one' (p. 64) and it is this borrowed identity that earns Rollo's approbation. Ten years earlier Olivia had failed to find in the glass the reflection she needed for reassurance, but now she has learned to adapt herself, at least outwardly, to the role she knows will please. This chameleon-like facility for adjusting to her surroundings does not, however, help her to solve the problem of the identity crisis that she is forced to confront once her love-affair with Rollo has acted as a catalyst.

This crisis is a symptom of the modern age that Lehmann here scrutinises, and it is not confined to women alone. Although extensive analysis of the male psyche is reserved for *The Echoing Grove*, and the guilt-ridden Rickie, destroyed by social pressures, there are suggestions in *The Weather in the Streets* that men as well as women are victims of their culture. Just as Olivia fails to fit into the niche that her elders think suitable, so her brother James appears as a young man who has similarly defied the promise of masculinity, refusing to follow in either of the career paths mapped out for him. As the only male Curtis of his generation, 'rebellious, not inclined to conform, to settle' (p. 37), he is admired by Olivia for his courage in adopting such a stance, though he is undoubtedly a disappointment to the rest of his family. Not only does James reject the two orthodox routes open to him – going to university or taking over the family business – but hints are given about the unhealthy tendencies of his artistic leanings, incompatible with the macho middle-class ethic. Looking round her brother's bedroom in the family home, Olivia notes that his books, his taste in music, the paintings are all the work of experimental artists. Just as throughout the novel rooms and houses denote a world of values, so artefacts also carry symbolic resonance. Here, Olivia recognises that these items, chosen so carefully by her brother, represent the struggle in which he has been engaged as a challenge to his heritage. In all her works, Lehmann demonstrates her awareness of gender stereotyping as it affects both men and women, and suggests the misery such social programming can produce. In this text the crises of masculinity are confined to the margins, though they are certainly present in hints – in James's untold story, in Ivor's confessions of weakness and, half-convincing though they are, even in Rollo's complaints about the pressures of his role as eldest son and his family responsibilities. But this is essentially a woman's story and it is the pressures on women to conform to preset models that are most centrally examined.

Yet in its portrayal of James and in the glimpses we are given of Olivia's friends, Anna and Simon, the novel displays characters who are engaged in the processes of creating their lives according to a scenario that has not been pre-programmed. James, whom Olivia discovers anew at the end of the book, deliberately rejects the narrative of the past whose plot he is asked to relive, opting instead for a route that is in direct opposition to the expectations of his elders. Anna, a photographer, and Simon, a painter, both creative artists, do not appear to have the same sort of past to slough off. They are inventors, starting afresh, working from the raw materials of experience to create something new and stimulating. In all her novels, Lehmann is fascinated by the idea of art as a powerful harmonising force, but also by its seductive quality, a feature that can prove dangerous. In *The Weather in the Streets* Anna's and Simon's homes convey this dualism. On the one hand they denote their inhabitants' vigour and their approach to existence as forward-looking and life-giving; on the other, they are the setting for sordid parties, where casual copulation, drunkenness and pretentiousness are rife. For the most part, however, they function as a positive counter to the dangerous thrall of the past. At dinner in Simon's studio, Olivia notices 'wherever the eye fell some mark of liveliness, some kind of wit, selection, invention – the vitality of shape, pattern, colour, making an aesthetic unity – the creative hand, the individual mind mattering' (p. 147). It is an image that stands in startling contrast to the rooms at Meldon, the home of Sir John and Lady Spencer that Olivia visits in the early chapters of the novel, rooms that rely on the heritage of the past for their effect, rooms packed with exquisite decorations and *objets d'art*, the products of a bygone age. It is only in retrospect that she realises that these rooms are 'dead, full of dead objects' (p. 147). Entering the drawing-room at Meldon for the first time for ten years, she is initially struck by its beauty and comforted by its sameness. Entering the second time, she is aware that 'the group by the fire had a static quality as if anaesthetized. . . . Time drew a circle round the scene. It was now: it was a hundred, two hundred years ago' (p. 97). It is a mark of Olivia's ambiguous position, caught half-way between two cultures, that she finds the Spencers both attractive, in the stability they offer, and inimical, in their resistance to change. For she recognises that they stand at the 'end of a chapter' of history, obsessed with the past and with outdated customs of etiquette that reveal their world as a privileged sham. While the Spencers' dinner-party relies on servants for its effectiveness, the scene at Simon's studio conveys an absorption in community. The participants here are

active, involved in cooking, in serving the dinner, in energising
the evening rather than in sitting passively to be waited on, bound
by formality and rules. 'Where was I between the two?', Olivia
asks herself (p. 152), as her liaison with Rollo removes her from
her own circle of friends, reminds her of her bond with the
Spencers and sharpens her sense of cultural dislocation.

For Olivia is poised between the two worlds: that of the past
and that of the new age to come. Her position during her visit to
Meldon seems curiously equivocal. 'Now all was presented as in
a film or a play in which one is at one and the same time actor
and infinitely detached spectator' (pp. 73–4), she observes at the
dinner-table. This ambivalence underpins the technique of the
novel. Olivia is both thoroughly immersed in the production of
the story as it plays itself out and fully cognisant of the way in
which events could be reinterpreted. The narrative method, combining exterior with interior consciousness, and the constant shift
in tones from comedy to serious urgency reinforces this idea.
Lehmann produces keen, acidic portraits of the Spencer family, of
the narrow horizons of the women, so protected from the un-
welcome realities of ordinary people by virtue of their aristocratic
cocoon; and comic vignettes of the men, connoisseurs of the finer
things in life, including women among their number. Although
Olivia is temporarily seduced by this world of the past, she
ultimately realises its treachery and duplicitousnss. But despite
her knowledge that 'these people are not my people' (p. 114), her
childhood roots prevent her from making a clean break with their
values. The same sort of ambiguity colours the presentation of
Anna and Simon's circle. This group of people, devoted to art, to
personalities and relationships, to attacking convention, is revealed in an alternative perspective as brittle and lacking stability.
The party at Simon's is squalid and disordered, its drunken members a caricature of Bohemian licence, their dialogue affected and
their behaviour flamboyant.

Olivia's dilemma is intensified by the constant references
within the novel to the personalities and activities of the work
that preceded it, *Invitation to the Waltz*. The minor as well as the
major characters from that novel, Miss Robinson, Major Skinner,
Timmy Douglas and the others, all reappear in *The Weather in the
Streets*, their personal histories impinging on the edges of Olivia's

consciousness and forcing her to reassess the validity of her memories. For Olivia realises that childhood experience has emotional and psychological reverberations, its place in the formation of personal identity irrevocable. Driving home from the Spencers, she is surrounded by nostalgia. 'All that was important: had made an experience of emotions more complex, penetrating and profound, yes than getting married' (p. 129). Similarly the men whom Olivia met at Marigold's coming-out party, Timmy, Peter Jenkin and Pongo, reappear in the cooler gaze of her more mature apprehension. Echoes of the earlier book fill the pages of *The Weather in the Streets*. Sir John Spencer's remark as he goes into the library, 'absent me from felicity' (p. 110), is a direct quotation from *Invitation to the Waltz*. Whereas there it was witty and ironic, a shared family joke, it is now charged with sadness, a hollow cliché and a reminder of times when Sir John was in control. Yet it also recalls the energy and humour of the man who has aged and become frail, and Olivia is temporarily attracted by these mementoes of past times.

The damaging nature of the society that haunts Olivia is made explicit through the portrayal of Lady Spencer, the matriarch whose dignity and self-possession Olivia both admires and fears. Her unashamed use of power to prevent Olivia from intruding into Rollo's marriage is evidence of the authority she assumes as her right, in the face of which Olivia is helpless. The scene when she visits Olivia to ask her to end the affair shows Olivia's vacillation between antagonism and affection, between defiance and fatalistic submissiveness, as she confronts a clearly hostile force. Lady Spencer has come prepared for action, her eyes, 'steady, ice-blue; dictator's eyes, fanatically self-confident, without appeal' (p. 272). For the older woman, protecting the interests of her tribe, carries with her the full force of the entire establishment structure, heartless, single-minded, its veneer of civility one of its strongest weapons, prepared to crush any individual who threatens to topple it. Faced with evidence of its strength, Olivia is powerless to resist.

For while Olivia can be clear-sighted and critical of the past, she is yet bound by its power in a way that she recognises James is not. 'He's broken the mould entirely we were all cast in', she reflects on her brother, meeting him unexpectedly at a London soirée. 'I might have but I couldn't: meeting everybody half-way, a foot all over the place, slipping up here and there' (pp. 357–8). Olivia represents the rootlessness of contemporary woman, caught midway between the world of measured Edwardianism and the post-war gaiety of Georgian England. Superficially emancipated by the new society, she remains fundamentally unaltered in her longing for stability as embodied by the past. Like Dinah in *The Echoing Grove* a generation later, Olivia is trapped by her romantic nature, simultaneously a product of her sexual psychology and her cultural inheritance. The final section of *The Weather in the Streets*, with its multiple images of loss, death and loneliness, accentuates the nature of the trap she is in. Rollo's accident and Simon's death reveal to Olivia the extent of her isolation, her exclusion from community and family and her own emotional torpor. The final moments of the novel confront her even more forcibly with her own loss of autonomy. Unable to resist Rollo's charm she finds herself falling once more into the familiar routine of the romance plot she had determined to abandon. Without enthusiasm, she succumbs to Rollo's wheedling assumptions, resignedly conscious of her complicity in her own destruction.

6

Narrative and Power:
The Ballad and the Source

'I could have listened all day to Mrs Jardine for the sheer
fascination of her style', declares Rebecca Landon in an early
chapter of *The Ballad and the Source* (p. 23). The remark under-
lines one of the major topics of investigation in the novel: the
dominance of art. The source of Sybil Jardine's charismatic
personality, the pivot of the novel, is her 'style', a style that incorporates both verbal fluency and visual effect. For Sybil makes
herself into a work of art – the 'Enchantress Queen in an antique
ballad of revenge' (p. 238) – and it is the examination of the
compelling nature of narrative in particular as well as with power
relations in society that this novel concerns itself. Although Rosamond Lehmann's earlier work clearly pays attention to the
question of forms of dominance, especially in its social and sexual aspects, *The Ballad and the Source* takes the topic a stage
further in its parallel concern with forms of artistry: theatrical,
visual, literary. In its special concentration on the power of narrative and in its construction of a series of Chinese boxes of
stories within the main story, the book creates a sequence of elaborate puzzles that form a comment on their own artifice. In this
sense the novel seems to anticipate the work of later twentieth-
century writers whose post-modernist questioning of the nature of
narrative exhibits itself in the ludic self-reflexivity of their fictive
structures. In addition, in its focus on oral narrative and on stories
told by, about and to women, *The Ballad and the Source* examines the mythic status of such tales and the ways in which a
female narrative inheritance is constructed and continued through

an oral tradition. The title of the work at once draws attention to
its subject: the tangled roots and the complexities of archetypal
forms of narrative and their relationship with human experience.

Several of Rosamond Lehmann's novels deal with the notion of
narrative compulsion. Their heroines, Judith Earle, Grace Fairfax,
Olivia Curtis, Rebecca Landon, Sybil Jardine, are imaginative
girls or women, who find in their fantasy lives a source of nour-
ishment and a means of escape from mundane and often
unpleasant reality. Lehmann also wrote a number of articles and
spoke widely about her own role as author, succumbing to the
potent fascination of story-telling. She once compared the writing
of a novel to a magical journey 'an absolutely new experience; an
undiscovered world whose unlikeness, not likeness, to any other
is the real reason for setting out to find it'.[56] Yet the 'undiscovered world' also has its foundation in the author's personal
memories. As Lehmann acknowledged in an interview,

> It does all come out of the unconscious, my unconscious,
> which is very well stocked – with images, memories, sounds,
> voices, relationships. There comes a moment when they seem
> to coalesce and fuse, and suddenly something takes shape, like
> seeing a whole landscape with figures, or a whole house with
> all its rooms.[57]

Of all Lehmann's works *The Ballad and the Source* draws most
strongly on autobiographical material in its portrayal of the child
narrator, Rebecca Landon. Sharing the same initials as her
creator, Rebecca is the second daughter in a family of four
children, three girls and a boy, who, like the Lehmanns, live in a
country house just outside London. Their father is a successful
man of letters; their mother comes from New England; and
Rebecca's birthdate is in 1902, just a year after Lehmann's own.
Rebecca had been used before by Lehmann in two short stories
based on incidents from her childhood, 'The Gypsy's Baby' and
'The Red-Haired Miss Daintreys', and she was to figure again as
the central character in her last completed novel, *A Sea-Grape
Tree*. In *The Ballad and the Source*, as the romantic little girl who
becomes engrossed in a world that is evoked for her at second
hand, she dramatises Lehmann's initiation into the world of

imaginative creation. Other figures too take their inspiration from real-life personalities remembered from Lehmann's childhood. Sybil Jardine's character grew from a story told to Lehmann about a great-aunt who had disgraced the family by abandoning her husband and child for a lover, and who, like Sybil, tried desperately to recover the child she was subsequently prevented from seeing. Like Sybil, she tried to manipulate others, including Lehmann herself as a child, to help her achieve her goal. Similarly, Tilly, the dwarfish seamstress who has been privy to the past histories of both Sybil and the Landons, is based on the 'tiny black antique fairy, almost a midget, in the sewing room'[58] at Bourne End, one Mrs Slezina, who was the source of a fund of stories about Rosamond Lehmann's grandmother in her youth. The novel is set in a period that corresponds to the years when Lehmann herself was growing up, and Rebecca, like her creator, is a young teenager at the outbreak of war. Echoes of certain descriptive passages in the book can even be found in Lehmann's autobiographical accounts of her early life. It is as if the collusion between reality and imagination, so strong a theme in the novel, has already begun with its author's choice of subject matter. As Rosamond Lehmann remarked in *The Swan in the Evening*, it is 'difficult if not impossible to disentangle "true" from "not true"'.[59] Her comment goes straight to the heart of *The Ballad and the Source.*

For in this novel the subject of narrative is intertwined with a moral enquiry, characteristic of British fiction of this period, into the social values of the age. In turn this is associated with an analysis of sexual politics and the unjust treatment of women. Through the historical perspective given by the text, the self-perpetuating nature of these issues becomes evident, and the socio-psychological aspects of gender and the female inheritance transmitted from generation to generation are shown to be archetypal features in stories from myth to the present day. The novel is woven around the figure of Sybil Jardine, whom we see through Rebecca's eyes. Sybil's story, as it gradually unfolds through a number of second-hand accounts, is the story of a woman who, having made a fatal error early in her life, now seeks revenge on the society that has let her down. In a flashback we are told how Sybil, a Victorian beauty of good family, married

young and had a daughter, Ianthe. Her marriage failed to satisfy
her and after her elopement with a lover, who subsequently
proved worthless, her husband refused to allow her access to their
child. Her rash action proves irredeemable, losing her not only
her husband and child, but also the friendship of the woman she
most cherished, Laura, the grandmother of Rebecca Landon. Yet,
despite being thwarted at every turn, Sybil remains driven by her
obsessive need to reclaim her daughter and to re-establish her
own social position. It is only after her husband's death that she
ultimately meets Ianthe again, to discover that the baby she had
loved has grown into a young woman who detests her. The rest of
her life is spent trying to recapture these lost relationships, and
especially to re-establish the bond between mother and daughter
that has been denied her. When Rebecca meets her, Sybil is an
elderly and embittered woman, attempting to reconstruct the past
through the youth of a new generation: Ianthe's three children and
the Landon girls, Laura's grandchildren. As the novel develops,
Rebecca observes at first hand Sybil's strategies as she tries to
bend others to her will, and herself falls under the spell of Sybil's
undeniable charm. Rebecca also witnesses the present-day sequel
to the history that has so enthralled her, as a number of tragic
events befall Sybil, culminating in the final appearance of Ianthe,
distracted and suicidal, her life having repeated many of the circumstances of Sybil's own. The fascination exerted by these
characters inspired Lehmann thirty years later to write *A Sea-
Grape Tree*, a book that takes the story a stage further to build,
again via a flashback technique, the chain of events leading to
Sybil's death. In this short novel, the leitmotif patterning found in
The Ballad and the Source is given its coda, as the violence and
tragedy that form the climax to the earlier work are shown to
wind down in a subdued, but not final, resolution.

In many respects *The Ballad and the Source* continues to explore a number of issues that are central to Lehmann's earlier
novels. In particular it is concerned with the relationship between
gender and power in its presentation of a woman who has sinned
against an implacable patriarchal society and finds that all
avenues of hope are consequently closed to her. By showing Sybil
as an ageing heroine at the start of the story, Lehmann is able to
use a retrospective narrative technique to point up the determinis-

tic processes of history. For unlike Lehmann's other works this is a historical novel, set in the past, looking back to a Europe and a way of life that has long disappeared. Sybil is a Victorian woman who challenges the conventions of that hidebound society. In following her story through to its bitter end, Lehmann plots the changes in social attitudes that span the turn of the century and the shift from Victorianism to a modern-day society. The past always operates as a compelling force in Lehmann's fiction and it is recalled here as a vital window on the present. It is only by understanding history, the text implies, that one can arrive at self-recognition. So Rebecca Landon is introduced in the context of her family, her own abilities measured against those of her ancestors.

> Although unmusical, and for that reason a disappointment, something we felt, might be done with writing? – drawing? – acting? . . . We would be three brilliantly talented sisters, as in the generation before us, and the one before that. Yet sometimes a doubt blew across this simple optimistic programme. That mint was abandoned, the coins passing out of currency. (p. 13)

The modern girl that is Rebecca is significantly different from her forebears, and her personal uncertainties have their source in her awareness of her affinities with the past. Seeking to find herself, she needs first to comprehend her heritage and to identify her own point of departure from the traditional model. Similarly the novel has its basis in nineteenth-century fictional antecedents but revises and departs significantly from these. Lehmann's debt to her novelistic predecessors is most evident in the tales of Sybil's youth, for just as *The Weather in the Streets* provided an exposure of the romance genre, so *The Ballad and the Source* is fashioned to form a parody of the popular forms of Victorian sensation fiction. The figures in the story – the unforgiving husband, the woman with a secret, the abandoned child – are stock characters from melodrama, and their actions and situations repeat the habituated conventions found in the novels of popular writers of that period. Indeed Sybil's situation is seen simultaneously in highly exaggerated and starkly realistic terms. The oblique narrative method self-consciously recalls theatrical excess: the language used by the narrators, Sybil, Tilly and Rebecca, is frequently florid and the plot mechanisms hackneyed. At the same time these features are counterbalanced by the glimpses of real suffering and social commentary the text offers, for Sybil, as the heroine of a real-life drama, embodies the dilemma of the passionate individual born into a society that cannot accommodate her needs. The stories of Ianthe and of Maisie, Sybil's daughter and granddaughter, intertwined with the main narrative strand, both repeat and diverge from that of Sybil herself to show the patterning of female history and its cyclical nature.

The vision of the past that is ultimately realised in this novel has none of the sentimentality it is accorded via the recollections of the fictional characters, Tilly and Sybil. From between the lines of the exaggerated accounts of those personally involved in the drama emerges a picture of a rigid social structure that makes no allowances for women and their need for expression. Sybil is a sexually frustrated heroine, trapped in a marriage that has failed to fulfil its promise. As Tilly earthily puts it, 'What she wanted was a flesh and blood man . . . with a bit less in the attics and a bit more in the basement' (p. 64). Yet she is also seduced by the promise of romance to leave the security of her home for what proves to be an illusory ideal. In following her natural desires and eloping with her lover, Sybil forfeits her marriage and consequently all her legal rights within Victorian society. The clash between the mutually exclusive sets of values possessed by Sybil and her husband is reflected in the terminology they adopt to deal with one another. Sybil's is the language of emotion. She appeals to integrity and a sense of honour. She makes reference to love, to trust and to humanity. Her husband, Charles Herbert, on the other hand falls back on legal phrasing. The law protects his position and denies his wife any standing. He is able to dictate terms to Sybil and threatens her with police arrest if she should attempt to see her baby. Rebecca's spontaneous reaction to the story – 'How could he? She was hers just as much as his' (p. 75) – demonstrates the tension present throughout the novel between natural and social justice. As Sybil claims in her attempts to see her daughter, 'I've not come to steal her or corrupt her. This is right. This is just. This is human. Not the law of cruel men. The law of humanity. My own child!' (p. 88). But Charles Herbert, the representative of the patriarchal order with his wealth, status and authority, is shown as holding all the cards. Not only does he deny Sybil her home and child, he makes it impossible for her to live within the country or be a part of the society whose codes of behaviour she has violated.

Sybil's helpless situation as a woman without legal redress emphasises the polarisation of male and female roles within the existing social structure, as she is progressively isolated from family and friends because of her anti-social actions. In placing the law of 'cruel men' against the law of 'humanity', the book sets up a conflict of interests between the social and the natural that is explored most fully in the analyses of parent–child relationships. Similarly, Laura, Rebecca's grandmother, finds herself caught between the demands of duty and of love when Sybil appeals to her for help. Laura's obligation to obey her husband and to deny Sybil access to her daughter forces her into an intolerable position where she must choose between her marriage and the friendship that means so much to her. *The Ballad and the Source* continues the interest in women's friendship that characterises other Lehmann works. The love between Judith Earle and Jennifer Baird in *Dusty Answer*, between Grace Fairfax and Norah Mackay in *A Note in Music*, and between the sisters Olivia and Kate Curtis in *Invitation to the Waltz* all suggest the depth of the undercurrent of female bonding. In *The Ballad and the Source* the relationship between Rebecca and Maisie is seen as a regenerative echo of the love that existed between their grandmothers and, like the alliances of the earlier novels, it testifies to the nourishing mutual rapport that can exist between women. The affection between Sybil and Laura, however, ultimately subversive in its tendencies, is forbidden to flourish in a society where men make the rules. Conversely men band together to protect their interests, and Laura's husband issues orders to his wife to uphold Charles Herbert's decisions, just as thirty years later, Rebecca's father maintains the rule of non-forgiveness when his wife would accede to Sybil's entreaties. As Sybil explains to Rebecca,

Do you know what goes to make a tragedy? The pitting of one individual against the forces of society. Society is cruel and powerful. The one stands no chance against its combined hostilities. But sometimes a kind of spiritual victory is snatched from that defeat. Then the tragedy is completed. . . . Yes. Love proposed. Man disposed between Laura and myself. (p. 108)

The fight between Sybil and her husband is not, then, just a conflict between two individuals, but one between female values and desires, and the entire patriarchal structure that conspires against them. The intimacy between Laura and Sybil, however profound its sympathy, is destroyed by the combined weight of the laws, codes and practices that inevitably intervene in their personal allegiance.

Sybil's feminist leanings and her attempts to take a stand for the rights of women result in her ostracism from polite society and her eventual expatriation. 'As a girl', Tilly tells Rebecca, 'she was always one to go on about women's rights – and they should all be trained up to perfessions like men, and be the equal of 'em' (p. 89). Tilly's contempt for Sybil's militancy contains an implicit acceptance of the impossibility of such an argument. Images of women's captivity recur in the novel. The limits on Ianthe's freedom of movement are emphasised when Charles Herbert places bars on the windows of his house, an ambivalent gesture of protection that reinforces her real status as prisoner. 'She was trapped', insists Sybil, speaking about her daughter's adolescence, 'She must be released – no matter how' (p. 152). The misplaced security that men offer women contributes to a repressive environment that results in metaphorical and literal female sterility, producing creatures who are afraid to confront reality or to explore their own potential. Ianthe, brought up without a mother, in the devoted gaze of her elderly father, grows up self-absorbed, in 'a room of mirrors . . . afraid of the world' as people who 'dare not look outward for fear of getting too much hurt' (p. 119). The description is strikingly similar to that given of Sybil Jardine who 'gets back – *immeasurable* reflections of herself' from all points of her experience. At the end of the novel, Ianthe, despairing and close to madness, is confined behind a locked door, an ironic counterpoint to the blue door in the wall

behind which Mrs Jardine lives. For Sybil, like the classical figure for which she is named, always retains a static quality in spite
of her dynamism. Throughout the many scenes in which she
appears, she is most often associated with interiors and enclosed
spaces, whether a walled garden, a boudoir or a French chateau,
and when seen in the outside world, she remains half concealed,
wrapped in a cloak or heavily veiled, uncomfortable in a setting
where she is not in supreme control.

The power structures in the culture that victimises Sybil force
her to seek a refuge that becomes both a sanctuary and a power
centre. Paradoxically, Sybil's retreat from English society allows
her access to a personal space from which she can plot her
revenge on the system that has banished her, bringing her agents
within her reach to try to manipulate them to her will. The child
Rebecca Landon, unsuspectingly caught in this web, finds herself
playing her part in the grand design that Sybil Jardine has woven.
'What a little *dea ex machina* you are proving' (p. 103), Sybil
tells her, as Rebecca unwittingly discloses information that the
adult world had deliberately kept hidden from her. Like the Greek
drama to which it makes continual reference, the novel moves towards its inexorable resolution of death and destruction along the
lines of a familiar narrative scenario. The characters become
pawns in the game that Sybil has devised for them, working
through a tragic plot that is not of their choosing. Sybil Jardine
uses art to gain power, and the battle that she is engaged in is
fully recognised as such by all who encounter her.

The military imagery that permeates the novel reinforces the
idea of warfare on both a domestic and an international scale.
'Mrs Jardine had been carried off the field, but the day was hers:
no doubt of that', notes Rebecca from her position of spectator of
the 'fight of Maisie for Cherry's soul' (p. 34). Sybil's approach to
situations is that of a soldier, marshalling her weapons to retain
control or to extend her territory. Her husband, Harry Jardine, the
embodiment of Victorian militarism, provides an ironic complement to the personal battle in which his wife is engaged. He
represents the gentlemanly code of behaviour in war, where the
ground-rules are perfectly understood and the terrain of encounter
mapped out in advance. The outbreak of the First World War,
which occurs half-way through the present-day action of the

novel, adds a further dimension to the military refrain, and incidentally strengthens the theme of period change introduced at the outset of the work. The Great War takes place on a very different sort of battlefield from that where Harry Jardine fought. Rather it is one where the old rules are discarded and young men, such as Malcolm Thomson, are slaughtered in an arbitrary fashion. As a war where there are no triumphant victories or glorious heroes in the old style, the image of the First War reinforces the sense of moral confusion that for Rebecca seems to characterise the contemporary generation. The military events of the masculine political world thus not only provide a context for the psychological and emotional conflict in which women engage, but also recall the historical subject that creates a framework for the book as a whole.

But the novel is not purely a study in power relations. It is equally the story of Rebecca Landon's emergent consciousness as she is made accessory to an adult world of intrigue and sexual machinations that she cannot fully comprehend. It is Rebecca's involvement in the story that reveals its true complexity. The complicated narrative structure and her position within it point up the self-conscious artifice of the text and its self-reflexive concern with the seductive quality of story-telling itself. The opening of *The Ballad and the Source* re-creates a characteristic Lehmann situation, that of the imaginative child about to enter a new world through her encounters with the family, both glamorous and dangerous, who live in the house next door. 'The blue door in the garden wall' (p. 7) is the image that inspires the novel, and the longing to see through to the other side is the corollary to the prosaic world that we all inhabit. With the contrast between the poetic excess of Mrs Jardine's letter inviting the children to tea, and Mrs Landon's dull translation of it, the appeal of romantic narrative is made apparent, and this movement between the two modes of discourse establishes the novel's different 'worlds', which Rebecca must negotiate. Sybil's letter, her personal charisma and the tales of her past life awaken Rebecca to the existence of a level of experience beyond the normal routine of daily life, and like all Lehmann heroines she finds it irresistible. As Mrs Jardine invites Rebecca into the world that she has fabricated, she takes on the role of the enchantress she is subsequently compared with, transforming facts as she rewrites her life according to the fictional models she has inherited from classical and romance literature. Rebecca is readily drawn into the magic of the creation. As she explains towards the end of the novel, 'It was like hearing something so true it made everything else I knew or that I'd been taught – seem like – boring feeble pretence' (p. 240). In submitting to the overwhelming magnetism of the stories she hears, Rebecca acknowledges the power of art, which reverses and revises our conceptions of the world. Yet she remains a perennial outsider: she only experiences events at a remove, and so is always distanced from them. It is only in the sequel to this novel, *A Sea-Grape Tree*, that she too becomes a participant, acting out the romantic fantasy that Sybil herself was unable to consummate.

Significantly, at the first meeting with Mrs Jardine, Rebecca is a child, who, like other Lehmann children, retains 'the faculty for pure immediate awareness' (p. 248) which dissipates in later life. One of the novel's concerns is with the act of recollection itself, whether it be via the story-telling of the narrators – Tilly, Sybil and Maisie – or whether it be through Rebecca's attempts to reconstruct the magical atmosphere of her childhood. At the beginning of chapter IV the adult Rebecca describes the impressionistic nature of memory in a passage that can be taken to encapsulate the technique not only of this novel but of all Lehmann's fictions about childhood.

> Looking back into childhood is like looking into a semi-transparent globe within which people and places lie embedded. A shake – and they stir, rise up, circle in interweaving groups, then settle down again. There are no dates. Time is not movement forward or backward through them, but simply that colourless globe in which they are all contained. Adolescence coalesces in a separate globe; heavier, more violent and confused in its agitations when shaken. (p. 27)

Nostalgia constitutes a creative act, imposing a pattern on the past that defies chronology and establishes its own internal logic. Rebecca herself is a catalyst, facilitating the memories of others in *The Ballad and the Source*, a filter who revivifies dormant life

in *A Sea-Grape Tree*. Her role accords with Lehmann's view of
the author's function as essentially passive,

> actively passive, with mind and senses at full stretch, incorpor-
> ating, selecting, discarding; in fact abandoned – not to
> sanctimonious looseness – but to every unbargained-for, yet
> acceptable, inevitable possibility of fertilization.[60]

At the bizarre dinner-party held in the Jardines' deserted
country house on Christmas Eve 1916, the setting and the other
characters appear to Rebecca as if 'in a flickering surrealist film
sequence' (p. 231), hazy and intermittent, just as Lehmann
describes the authorial act as 'a detached condition' such as 'one
gets at the cinema'.[61] The clarity of the imagery that Rebecca
absorbs in the early stages of the novel becomes more diffuse as
she enters adolescence and the moral direction consequently less
certain. The sharply defined figures of good and evil as they
emerge from the sagas told by Tilly and Mrs Jardine become less
easy to categorise towards the end of *The Ballad and the Source*.
'My reverence for art was intense but incoherent', Rebecca
concedes, still as passionate as in the uncritical years of her
childhood, but less confident about her ability to judge the moral
complexities she encounters from the simple perspective of childhood.

The subject of the moral dimension of art is introduced early in
the novel with the portrayal of Maisie, ever the pragmatist even
as a twelve year old. The obvious Jamesian parallels – the child's
innocent exposure to the scheming of adults and her use as a
counter in their antagonistic games – seem to culminate in a
deliberate reminder of the original in *What Maisie Knew*, with the
choice of Maisie as a child whose moral righteousness remains
untainted by the corruption she witnesses. But unlike her precursor, Maisie in *The Ballad and the Source* is highly partisan. To
her, romance is nothing more than a form of deceit, a distorting
gloss on the realities of life. Having been brought up in an
environment of strict Scots Presbyterianism, she is pugnaciously
resistant to the captivating wiles of Mrs Jardine, for as she confides to Rebecca, her father has 'told me she's a liar. And she
made my mother a liar. He said if he ever caught any of us lying

he'd whip us within an inch of our lives' (p. 48). The sentiment is echoed in Tilly's story of the child, Ianthe, warned by her father against the mother whose beauty and charm masks deception. 'It seemed', muses Rebecca, 'that this thing went on and on like a curse. Liar begot liar; and all their road forward and back, far back, was cratered with disastrous pits of guilt, haunted by ruinous voices crying vengeance' (p. 82). This sense of the moral dualism that art generates is examined in one of Lehmann's best-known short stories, written about the same time as *The Ballad and the Source*. In 'The Gypsy's Baby', Rebecca's neighbour, the poverty-stricken child, Chrissy Wyatt, after a visit to tea, concocts a story about the Landons that represents their comfortable, middle-class home as a prison and their lives as joyless. Rebecca, shocked, is treated to a new perspective on the life she had taken for granted. Chrissy's stories take a more sinister turn when she subsequently invents a tale about the discovery of a child's body, a fabrication that leads to the arrest of a man for murder. The story turns on the issue of criminal responsibility as much as on the issue of childish fantasising. So, in *The Ballad and the Source*, Rebecca finds herself in a 'moral fog' as a direct result of the insights she is granted into the adult world, and in suggesting the narrow boundary between art and delusion, the text creates a complicated network of references that collaboratively illustrate the difficulties of defining objective truth.

This sense of the illusory nature of art is endorsed by the plethora of both literary and visual references in the text. The female characters in particular are measured against artistic models that glamorise fact. According to Tilly, Sybil is 'a picture' (p. 59), but on their first visit to the Jardines' home, Rebecca wonderingly compares the full-length portrait of Sybil as a young woman with the ageing figure who is before her. Similarly the miniature of Ianthe is turned into an iconic object in Maisie's reverential treatment.

Long curving neck. Bare shoulders, bosom swathed in blue chiffon. Dark hair elaborately piled and puffed out in lateral wings. Eyes painted a melting violet, skin snow-white with faintest wild-rose cheeks. She smiled mysteriously. She was Mrs Darling. She was a French New Year card angel-face, set

in tinsel and blossoms. She was every child's dream of a
romantic mother. (p. 52)

Just as Sybil's delicate beauty masks her strength and independent
nature, so Ianthe signally fails to live up to the promise of her
portrait. Despite Maisie's memory of her as being 'exactly like
that', Ianthe was no paradigm of maternal perfection but an adul-
teress who deserted her children in a repeat performance of her
own mother's abandonment of her baby. Despite herself, Maisie is
guilty of confusing the image with the reality, her memory just as
susceptible as the others to selective recollection of experience.
The dangers of failing to distinguish between art and life, an error
that a number of characters in this novel are guilty of, are given
tangible form at the end of the book when Ianthe mistakes the
sculpted models of Sybil and Cherry for the human beings they
represent, a mistake that leads to her breakdown and death.

Art, however, is mesmeric, and adults as well as children are
drawn within its grasp, both as recipients or practitioners. Tilly,
for instance, is a consummate artist, a story-teller of the highest
calibre. Herself a parody of a Dickensian fictional figure, she
shares with Sybil the task of interpreting the past and bringing it
to life in the present. In some respects she resembles Emily
Brontë's Nellie Dean, the imperfectly sighted narrator of *Wuthering Heights*, who from her privileged position as servant within
the household presents the events of the family to a fascinated but
innocent listener. Like *Wuthering Heights*, *The Ballad and the
Source* is shot through with refracted perspectives. In part this
connects with the theme of ageing and the shifting nature of
identity that is so strong in this novel. Laura, for example, can
only appear to the child, Rebecca, in the form of second-hand
accounts, often mutually exclusive. She is 'modest, self-confident;
sheltered, independent; despotic matriarch, young girl pliant and
caressing; fragility, energy with a core like the crack and sting of
a whip' (p. 15). These paradoxes attest to both the essential
mutability of the personality and the various and subjective impressions of the observers. 'Obviously no person was one and
indivisible – one unalterable unit – but a multiplicity', realises
Rebecca, contemplating the moral paradox that this involves, for
'everything about a person might be equally true and untrue' (p.

122). So the different names adopted by Sybil (Anstey, Jardine, Herbert) reflect the different parts she is required to play in life as well as endorsing this essential elusiveness in individual identity. Significantly, in *A Sea-Grape Tree* the adult Rebecca conceals her true identity from strangers. Taking the name Anonyme or No Name, she adopts an archetypal role, playing out a common female fantasy in her discovery of romantic bliss in an idyllic setting, timeless and undisturbed.

In her role as story-teller, Tilly demonstrates not only the power of narrative to rekindle the past but the influential role of the narrator in transforming those events. Tilly is 'a . . . medium reproducing skeleton dramas over and over again. The body of human life was drained out, yet a mystery, another piercing reality remained' (p. 61). In Tilly's version of the past, art has superseded reality, for as memories are filtered through a dramatised retelling of events, so the events themselves become elusive and fiction emerges as the only truth available. Tilly's language, melodramatic and clichéd, discloses her self-conscious artistry. She is a performer, an adept at dramatic monologues who casts the people she has known as stock characters from popular Victorian sensation literature. The society beauty, the innocent bride, the adoring lover, the errant wife, the proud father, the heartless husband all reappear in her view of the fashionable *beau monde*. The deliberate theatricality of her performance is a central feature of her stories. 'She had no intention of destroying her suspense to gratify a child's banal curiosity' (p. 63), observes Rebecca, enthralled by the production, as Tilly rolls her eyes stagily at climactic moments of her tale. Like any other artist, Tilly is in full control of her material, shaping it along the lines of well-known plots to create the effects she desires. The listener too has her part to play in this conspiracy and Rebecca is made aware of the responsibilities encumbent upon the audience. 'No feed line occurred to me', she confesses as Tilly pauses during a stage in the recounting (p. 62). But art is seductive. Tilly's speeches 'penetrated me like a probe, exploring depths that terrified me', Rebecca admits, begging for more despite her fear of the knowledge that is to come.

More sophisticated in her techniques than Tilly, Sybil Jardine too is an accomplished actress, so practised in her performance that it is difficult both for her and others to distinguish between truth and artifice in her character. Significantly, after the break-down of her marriage (in itself a virtual parody of a stage plot), she joins the professional theatre for a time. She also becomes a novelist, writing a thinly disguised autobiographical novel, 'the intimate life story of a wronged woman' (p. 91), presenting the events of her marriage in sensational form. As befits a former actress and writer, Sybil's professional narrative voice spills over into her attempt to manage life and Rebecca is constantly aware of her artifice at the same time as being spellbound by it. 'I was aware through all my being of her plan, her timing' (p. 98), says Rebecca with a mixture of admiration and suspicion. Mrs Jardine is both Prospero and military commander, devising strategies as self-defence and pursuing them relentlessly through carefully stage-managed scenarios.

As Rebecca becomes enmeshed in the narrative, both its com-plexity and its formal patterning become apparent to her. The elements that go to make up the story are referred to other, older narrative forms, which provide a backdrop for the contemporary action. As Sybil Jardine tells it, Ianthe's story replays the features of a range of different fictional modes, including myth, fable and classical tragedy. Ianthe and her father live together 'in the man-ner of a dispossessed monarch and his princess daughter' (p. 117). Ianthe is a 'rarely guarded creature . . . the casket of treasures' (p. 129) as well as a 'Snow-white Virgin, his dedicated Lamb, his unspotted Bride' (p. 117), the interweaving of fairy-tale, biblical and primitive folk motifs suggesting the archetypal nature of the tale that Sybil elaborates. Her theatrical presentation, with its melodramatic references and stylised language, produces the im-pression of a legendary world, in which the real-life people she refers to are accorded a classical status. Listening to her, Rebecca can only place the events of Ianthe's childhood and adolescence in the realm of myth. Despite the reassuring surroundings of the comfortable loggia with its basket chairs and gaily coloured cushions, Rebecca compulsively 'averted my eyes from the sky where, so it seemed, [Sybil's] fabulous gaze rested upon portents and monsters. Another moment and its candid and impenetrable depths would be rent for me – me too; some dire apparition, some mythical reptile would appal my sight' (p. 123).

It is an effect that Sybil deliberately encourages. She builds her family history within the pre-existing genres of classical tragedy and legend, making continual reference to those models. 'We chose always to live at the tragic level', she tells Rebecca, as she stands framed against a window, while like a stage-managed scenic effect 'a faint wind began to agitate the listening room, breathing upon us through the open pane the first premonitory chill of autumn' (p. 145). As she continues to present the lives of those around her as driven by fate towards their inexorable destiny, it is as if she is trying to absolve herself from responsibility in their plight. She too is a tragic victim, doomed to act out a predestined course, after the forces of an implacable society have proved too strong for her. 'Sometimes I seem to see us all as taken charge of', she tells Rebecca. 'The stage set and empty, the threads drawn all together, the knot tied' (p. 152). Critics have previously commented on the wealth of classical allusion in the novel, though they attribute different meanings to it. Sydney Janet Kaplan, for example, in a discussion of the mother and child motif, argues convincingly that the Demeter and Persephone myth is at the root of the text, and notes most interestingly the parallels between the role of Sybil Jardine and that of her classical namesake, the Sibyl of Cumae.

> The Sibyl, hung in a jar, responds to the children who ask her what she wants, 'I wish to die.' This is the Sibyl who led Aeneas to the underworld, where his spirit was restored and his dedication to his mission renewed. Now, in a degenerate time, her powers limited, she can only wish for death . . . the old rituals of renewal, like the Sibyl who once assisted in their performance, have been tainted by the weakness and corruption of man.[62]

The quotation directs us to the narrative act as much as towards the theme of the degenerative nature of power. The Sibyl, now immobile after a life of activity, is consigned to answering the enquiries of curious children, just as Sybil Jardine pours her efforts into explaining the past to Rebecca. The enigmatic quality of her role remains, however, exerting its uncanny effects on those whom she tries to influence, a representation of the forces of good corrupted by the bitterness of her experience. To Maisie, Sybil is 'an avenging Fury' (p. 268), waiting malignantly for her plans to come to fruition. For Gil, the young sculptor, she is the high priestess who should officiate at his wedding, her prophecies ensuring immortality for him and his bride (p. 233). Even to the child, Rebecca, she appears 'venomous' (p. 129) and 'serpentine', (p. 135), while still compelling her attention. The numerous references to Sybil's dramatic talent emphasise the theatrical aspect of her position. She can adapt her style at will, just as she can change her personality. As Rebecca observes, when Mrs Jardine is reproducing Tilly's version of events, 'It was as if the ghost pattern of Tilly's features kept intruding, diffusing Tilly's alien spirit through her own mask of flesh' (p. 170). In recalling the past, Sybil revises it according to the rhetorical models that seem most appropriate, and Rebecca's task is to unravel the truth from the confusing images with which she is confronted.

Sybil's dramatic method also enables her to find within her own family history significant parallels with classical and tragic literature that together illuminate the archetypal nature of the relationships she describes. At the heart of her tale, as Kaplan has observed, is an analysis of the fraught psychological bond between parent and child. Sybil's dark hints of an unhealthy and perverted love between Ianthe and her father refer the story back to the incestuous relationships central to classical tragedy and to Greek myth. The unnatural closeness between father and daughter results in Ianthe's emotional sterility, and in her being doomed to repeat the pattern of her own mother's experience, as she abandons her children and gradually declines into madness. Ianthe is perhaps the most vulnerable of all the characters in the novel: she lacks the inner resources that sustain Sybil, and is subject to male control without ever realising it. In *The Ballad and the Source* Lehmann uses a combination of literary and mythic parallels to evoke the psychological and social constraints on women, and to show the repetitive and cyclical nature of female history.

The central motif of the novel, that of thwarted mother and daughter relationships, has both classical origins and contemporary relevance in understanding the social legacy that women have inherited. The obsessional quest for Ianthe that motivates Sybil Jardine's actions is refracted through repeated images of lost children and unnatural family relations, framed by the norm of Rebecca's experience. The deaths of Tilly's son, the 'Little Feller', and of Ianthe's first-born provide tragic resonance to the main narrative strain, which shows a family broken and doomed to repeat the pattern of desertion. The sudden illness and arbitrary death of Cherry, the beautiful grandchild whom Sybil loves in place of her daughter, is read by Sybil as a forcible reminder of her own sterility, as if her single original error has barred her for ever from the act of mothering. In this novel, encounters between mothers and daughters are travesties of the norm, fraught by the tensions that have been erected through years of non-communication. The reunions between first Ianthe and Maisie, and second Sybil and Ianthe in the desperate closing scenes of the book are reversals of both the natural order and the stereotyped reunion scenes of sensation literature. Ianthe looks to her daughter, Maisie, for protection, unable to give her any sign of the maternal succour that Maisie longs for. She regresses to a passive childlike state, cowering in fear of her own mother, Sybil, whose appearance inspires in her only hatred and violence. The psychologist, Nancy Chodorow, in what has become a deeply influential work for feminist critics, has argued that the relationship between mother and daughter is a vital factor in female development, forming a pre-Oedipal bond whose intensity remains with a growing girl into adulthood. This bond, she suggests, provides women with a source of emotional sustenance that is often denied them in the patriarchal culture. Women who seek a continuation of this nurturance in an adult heterosexual relationship and who are disappointed may turn to mothering as a means of satisfying their need for relating to others, a crucial stage in their realisation of a full identity.[63]

The Ballad and the Source examines the effect on Ianthe and on her children, Maisie and Cherry, of the withdrawal of maternal love at an early stage in their lives and the consequent personality disorders that develop. It also shows Sybil (and to a lesser extent Tilly) as women who exhibit the fundamental desire for mothering in order to fulfil a deep psychological need. Ianthe, deprived of female nurturing, and repressed in a male-dominated environment, becomes mentally unbalanced. Warped and self-absorbed, she loses her own potential for creating relationships and for

mothering, the effects of emotional dispossession persisting into a
third generation. As Sybil describes it,

> 'The source, Rebecca! The fount of life – the source, the quick
> spring that rises in illimitable depths of darkness and flows
> through every living thing from generation to generation. It is
> what we feel mounting in us when we say: "I know! I love! I
> am!"' . . . 'Sometimes,' she said, 'the source is vitiated,
> choked. Then people live frail, wavering lives, their roots cut
> off from what should nourish them. That is what happens to
> people, when love is betrayed – murdered.' (p. 101)

Sybil here is able to confront both her past and the future inheritance she has bequeathed to others. What had originated in her as
a power for good has been corrupted by the influence of male
authority and the interruption of the instinctive bond between
mother and child. Her daughter and granddaughters suffer accord-
ingly, having been refused the succour they required to grow into
whole and healthy personalities. Thus Maisie, also suffering from
the effects of maternal deprivation, clings fiercely to the image of
a fairy-tale mother, which is perfect only in its artistic representation. Maisie herself grows up feeling contempt for the world of
adult sexuality. 'I shall have a different sort of life from other
people', she tells Rebecca at the age of seventeen, 'I shall never
fall in love' (p. 227). Her aberrant experience of family life and
her premature exposure to sexual squabbles result in her withdrawal from situations where she too might be vulnerable. In *A
Sea-Grape Tree* Rebecca is allowed to glimpse Maisie's adult life
and her attempts to establish a symbiotic relationship with her
own daughter, Tarni, significantly a child without a known father.
Yet the all-female world that Maisie tries to establish for Sybil's
great-granddaughter is also incomplete. In the photograph that
Rebecca sees of mother and child, Tarni 'wears the maniacal
expression of a being helplessly, ferociously at odds with circumstance' (p. 59), as her mother tries to shield her from the world of
men.

Lehmann's fiction has consistently dealt with the subject of the
family, and with the anxieties, jealousies and tensions that germi-
nate beneath the surface of harmonious living. Her heroines,

while isolated, or even, like Sybil Jardine or Dinah in *The Echoing Grove*, punishingly excluded from the communal experience, are repeatedly drawn to their family roots, gaining succour from the inextricable ties established in infancy. In Lehmann's work this ambivalence characterises women's links with family, whether in the role of daughter, wife or mother. In *The Ballad and the Source* the memorial to Cherry, sculpted by Gil, becomes the ultimate expression of all anguished mother–child relationships, representing both the intimacy and the unspeakable suffering of this deepest of bonds. The twin images of artistic and maternal creativity that so intrigued other women writers of this period, including Rebecca West and Elizabeth Bowen, and that find their antecedents in the work of Virginia Woolf and Katherine Mansfield, are closely paralleled in Lehmann's presentation of the links between narrative and motherhood. It is not incidental that all the narrators of *The Ballad and the Source* are women, or that the tale they are telling is to a young girl who gains from it her first insights into adult dissonance. *The Ballad and the Source* is Lehmann's most searching examination of the subject of female creativity in its various forms and the complicated inheritance it generates.

7

Realism and Reality

'This might be the line to pursue: to see one reality and turn it inside out again and again, making of one many, and all conflicting; and ending with a question mark.' So reflects a character in *A Note in Music* (p. 153), neatly summarising the technique that underlies the novel. The focus on subjective experience that dominates Lehmann's writing in all its forms inevitably invites a questioning of the concept of objective truth, but it is not until Rosamond Lehmann's last two major fictional works, *The Ballad and the Source* and *The Echoing Grove*, that this questioning becomes the central matter of the piece in question. As *The Ballad and the Source* indicates, with its dazzling maze of narratives overlaid one against the other, story-telling is a mechanism that helps to stimulate the act of memory and simultaneously exposes us to the confusing nature of events and their interpretation. *The Echoing Grove*, by taking a crucial episode in the lives of three characters and by retelling the story from each of their perspectives, reinforces and extends that confusion. It differs considerably from *The Ballad and the Source* by shifting attention from the theatricality of presentation that sets the tone for the earlier novel to a much more realistic and searching analysis of personality, psychological motivation and human failing.

By the early 1950s, Rosamond Lehmann's own experience in the wake of two world wars had made her sceptical about the permanence of moral value and of social relations, and this scepticism sets the tone for *The Echoing Grove*, a novel that is more detached and cynical in its view of personal relationships than many of her previous fictions. It is also a book that deliberately abstains from and indeed inhibits conventional moral judgements

114

on its characters, whose behaviour frequently subverts expected social norms. Although the characters themselves might adopt a judgemental stance – Madeleine and Dinah, for example, criticise one another's actions and in turn assume moral superiority – the continual shift in narrative position invalidates such attitudes. Moral integrity, a favourite subject in the work of British writers of the 1950s, is here seen as a liability, a quality that if taken seriously, as in Rickie Masters's constant self-reproach, leads only to guilt, frustration and profound unhappiness.

Shortly after the end of the Second World War, Lehmann had commented on the ways in which writers responded to the current unsettling social and cultural climate, when,

> For the present most novelists are likely to turn back to the time when, the place where they knew where they were – where their imaginations can expand and construct among remembered scenes and established symbols, just as they mostly did during the period [of the war]. They will look to their youth . . . or they will invent allegories and fantasies.[64]

These two approaches, recollection and fantasy, inform the method of *The Ballad and the Source* where the central character, Sybil Jardine, is herself an artist, using the past as a basis for narrative fabrication. Juvenile reminiscence in Lehmann's work before the 1940s had always been used as a means of measuring present consciousness against past experience, a gauge of both personal and social development, and a nostalgic recall of the loss of innocence. *The Ballad and the Source*, a text whose argument with the past is conducted through a series of retrospective narratives, presents past time with the same sort of gloss that Lehmann accords it in the above quotation, as a refuge and source of moral certainty. *The Echoing Grove*, published in 1953, deals largely with more recent and more adult histories, its emphasis highlighting the uncertainties and sense of loss that afflicts the protagonists as they examine their separate and shared pasts. In this novel characters seek security in personal relationships but always with the sense that these can promise only a temporary haven in a world where moral and social codes are in disarray. The book is suffused with an atmosphere of despondency, the

external setting of dissolution in an England of the 1950s corresponding to the emotional climate of isolation and bitter
understanding that the characters ultimately accept.

During the early 1940s Rosamond Lehmann had produced several stories that reflected a society coping with the effects of war.
Published originally in her brother John's collections of *New
Writing* and later collected in *The Gypsy's Baby*, these portray
small rural communities where those left at home are desperately
struggling to maintain the semblance of normality and the routine
of everyday life in the face of abnormal circumstances. Both 'A
Dream of Winter' and 'When the Waters Came' suggest the unreality and the precariousness of experience, made sharper by the
overturning of normal structures of daily existence. 'A Dream of
Winter' depicts a woman ill with influenza, who from her sickbed
watches the work of a beekeeper who has come to destroy a
hibernating swarm of bees in the cavity wall of her house. In her
dreamlike, feverish state, his actions and the excitement of her
children around her seem to take place at a remove, and the disposal of the bees becomes an apt analogy for the facile 'negation
and destruction' that war encodes. A further story, 'When the
Waters Came', tells of a mother walking with her two children
through a village on the day of a thaw after heavy snows. When
her small daughter falls into the water cascading down the village
street, the mother moves in a controlled panic to the rescue,
which is quickly and easily effected. In each story the narrative
perspective is conditioned by bizarre circumstances – the feverish
illness that creates strange, phantasmagorical images; the extreme
weather that has altered the landscape and transformed roads into
rivers – to give a surrealistic effect, an impression of an environment where the overturning of life's regularities has become
unremarkable. A longer story, 'Wonderful Holidays', with its de-
tailed account of the attempts to mount a village concert in aid of
the war effort, accentuates this sense of coexistent fantasy and reality by creating a picture of a lop-sided community, a society
peopled by women, children, the elderly and the infirm. As com-
munications break down and frustrations accumulate, it is the
women who have to cope with the organisation of village events,
with food rationing, the bringing up of children and the pretence
at family life in the absence of male support. These stories evoke

a world temporarily thrown off balance, their naturalistic detail heightening rather than modifying their unnatural impact.

The Echoing Grove continues this same technique, using metonymic specificity to contribute to the feeling of disturbance in its portrayal of a society no longer sure of its moral and social parameters. The meticulous description of interiors of rooms, of streets and domestic surroundings as found in the short stories is augmented in the novel by references to actual London locations and historical events, but this accuracy only aggravates the sense of a world adrift, its characters searching for a point of anchor. In its probing of the sources and effects of contemporary displacement, the novel achieves a level of psychological realism not previously attempted in Lehmann's writing. At the same time, despite its concentration on individual experience, the interplay of continually shifting narrative perspectives undermines the fact and the validity of a single materiality or interpretation of events. The background of war, which provides a context for much of the story, heightens its hallucinatory aspect. In one central section of the novel, for example, Rickie, the aberrant husband, spends a night with Georgie, a woman whose own husband is away at the front. The impression created is that of a world of licence, an existence where peacetime rules are suspended and moral and personal codes of behaviour are reassessed. In the wartime night the blackout reigns, streets are in darkness, bombs fall while people shelter in the basements of buildings and above their heads their homes are shelled to ruins. In this context of arbitrary and imminent death, lovers are parted, disappearances into the unknown become a routine occurrence, and new relationships are formed without warning and with no insurance of future security.

Yet in this climate of cultural instability, remnants of the old values persist. *The Echoing Grove* takes a traditional subject, that of the family, on which to unfold its patterns of faithlessness, and it is a family that itself comes under intensive examination as a source of disjunction. Rosamond Lehmann's earlier fictions took as their focus the developing adolescent consciousness of her heroines, families functioning as a background for individual growth, or seen as a formidable power structure against which resistance must be marshalled. In *The Echoing Grove*, however, the family is no harmonious unit, where intimacies are established and parents are comforting, stable figures, nor is it a solid and impregnable fortress, but rather a battleground, where neuroses are engendered and marital tensions are rife. Within the Burkett family at the heart of the story, the two sisters, their parents, husbands and lovers, who form the nucleus of investigation, there is another familiar story enacted, that of the eternal triangle. Rickie Masters, married to Madeleine Burkett but deeply involved in a love-affair with her sister, Dinah, is the ostensible focus of the novel. The majority of the narrative, devoted to a penetrating analysis of the tortuous three-way relationship, emanates from his perspective. Unlike the complicated narrative ramifications of *The Ballad and the Source*, the novel that precedes it, *The Echoing Grove* is built around a tight and narrow structure, with little plot development. Rather it expands inwards in its extended exploration of the effects of adultery on the three participants, Rickie, Madeleine and Dinah. As Walter Allen has observed, the result is that of 'a suffocatingly claustrophobic work in which never for a moment are we allowed the least relief from the masochistic self-torture suffered by the principal characters'.[65] In this novel there is no filter, no child such as Rebecca Landon, through whose eyes adult passion can be mediated. The story of sexual intrigue, betrayal, guilt and bitterness is repeated in its differing versions through the internal recollections of the participants themselves, obsessed by the past which has conditioned their present circumstances.

Set a few years after the end of the Second World War, and dealing with protagonists who are now middle-aged, the book opens with an encounter between the two sisters, shortly after Rickie's death. From this vividly imagined external present, the narrative moves back in time to the crucial period of the long drawn-out affair between Rickie and Dinah during the 1930s and the exterior settings quickly give way to an equally graphic internal landscape, 'a desert, dry, limitless, bleached and blackened; banal as grief or death' (p. 135). The book is divided into sections, each of which corresponds to a time during the twenty-four-hour period when Madeleine and Dinah are together. As in Rosamond Lehmann's previous work, the act of memory is central to the novel as the protagonists reconstruct their separate narratives, each episode of recollection containing a span of time

that stretches back over thirty years, as the convoluted relationships are seen to be determined by the past and reconstituted by
memory which cannot be evaded.

This theme is made explicit in the opening pages of the novel,
when the sisters, meeting for the first time after a fifteen-year
separation, are compared to 'two people coming back to a
bombed building once familiar, shared as a dwelling, and finding
over all the smashed foundations a rose-ash haze of willow herb.
No more, no less. it is a ruin' (p. 13). Their dialogue, brittle and
nervous, covers unspoken thoughts and feelings, suppressing their
shared knowledge of the devastated emotional territory that lies
between them. As they take the dog for an afternoon walk
through the local churchyard, Madeleine and Dinah discover a rat,
which their dog has nosed out and attacked. Its determined and
bloody fight for survival compels the two women to come to the
dog's rescue and in trying to kill the rat, they engage in a metaphorical slaying of the poisonous memory that is gnawing away
at their own relationship. As they confront the rat's wounded and
pathetic body, its presence elicits profound emotions and the
sisters' unnaturally violent responses released by its death throes
resolve into a cathartic displacement of their unspoken feelings
about Rickie. Ugly, vicious and dangerous, the rat is the living
embodiment of the monstrous impulses within them that can only
be erased through confrontation. Surprisingly it is Madeleine, the
more conventional and placid of the two, who finally kills the
animal. Dinah, more volatile and unorthodox, cannot in the last
moments bring herself to strike the death blow. When, however,
she buries the body, it is as if the two sisters have shared equally
in the task of annihilation, an ultimately therapeutic process, for
the episode echoes the gradual erosion of Rickie himself, and
their tacit complicity in his death. As the impersonal narrator of
this first section observes, 'Darkness, close up this fissure; dust
under roots and stones, consume our virulent contagion; silence,
annul a mortal consternation. We must all recover' (p. 29). The
subsequent chapters comprise a process of disclosure, uncovering
the primitive emotions that lie buried within the metaphorical
fissure, a breach that is only sealed by the women's eventual
reconciliation. The novel's construction is a circular one, forming
a pattern of retrogression that then moves forward again towards

the sisters' reunion, the book's starting-point thus also constitut-
ing its ending.

This opening scene functions as a prelude for the psychological
action that occupies the substance of the work. Gradually the omniscient narrator is succeeded by a series of internal monologues
that move between the respective thoughts of the three characters
in the drama, with occasional insights into the perceptions of
minor figures. Technically *The Echoing Grove* is Rosamond
Lehmann's most ambitious novel, skilfully exploiting a range of
registers to dramatise the voices of both men and women, and to
delineate the differential psychology of personality. The book also
marks a departure for Lehmann in that the central section of the
narrative is devoted to a male rather than a female consciousness.
Rickie Masters, the adulterous husband, is a very different
portrait from Rosamond Lehmann's other philanderer, Rollo
Spencer, a man who limits women to their roles as sexual and
social companions. Unlike Rollo, Rickie is a sensitive and complicated human being, self-analytical, tortured by passion and
consumed by moral complexes, elements only obliquely suggested
in Rollo's portrayal in *The Weather in the Streets*. As a study of
the psychological effects of guilt, Rickie is an intricate creation
and the placing of his narrative at the centre of the novel provides
a formal complement to his position between the two women who
love him and who between them tear him apart.

The contrasts that Madeleine and Dinah embody are made evident at the beginning of the second section of the book,
'Morning', which opens with Dinah waking up in Madeleine's
spare room, after a fitful night's rest. As in *The Weather in the
Streets*, Lehmann takes the unorthodox as her starting-point. It is
the mistress, not the wife, who is the initial focus of sympathy,
her memories jogged by the photograph of Madeleine's daughter
to recall her own near-fatal experience of motherhood when she
gave birth to Rickie's stillborn child in snowbound conditions. In
these opening images, the central polarities of the text are made
explicit, the legitimate and illegitimate placed side by side, the
living daughter set against the dead son, 'lawful wedlock' against
the 'lawless dark', the wife against the mistress. Following in the
pattern of Lehmann's earlier heroines, Dinah is a rootless,
isolated character, a woman whose identity has been partially

destroyed by illicit love. Her years as Rickie's mistress seem in retrospect to be only wretched, 'nothing but wear and tear, concealment, lies, suspicion; only half a person' (p. 104). To some extent she is a natural development from the characterisation of Olivia Curtis, who, at the end of *The Weather in the Streets*, is left poised on a downward path, the little control she has over her life about to be taken from her. Dinah, however, is a more reckless character than Olivia, more outspoken in her rebellious stance and more determined to be her own woman. Despite the assurances given in the novel about her passionate nature, she lacks the spontaneity and warmth of heroines such as Judith or Olivia, and consequently she fails to engage the reader's sympathy in quite the same way.

Dinah's shabby London flat with its few possessions suggests the bleak and haphazard quality of her life. It stands in sharp contrast to Madeleine's homes, the comfortable country cottage that she now inhabits, and the elegant town house that she shared with Rickie. Yet Dinah's position of exclusion from a conventional lifestyle is largely self-imposed and she does not regret her rebellious stance. At the end of the novel, thinking back over her life, she ascribes her attitude to jealousy. 'I couldn't compete in your world', she tells Madeleine. 'And you made it so plain I wasn't really acceptable' (p. 282). Dinah's attribution of the source of her disaffection to family friction is borne out by the encounter between Dinah and her mother in 'Nightfall'. Here the atmosphere is fraught with generational tensions, and both the spoken dialogue and the internal thoughts of the two women suggest the gradual displacement of both feeling and value-systems that leads to reserve between parent and child. As Mrs Burkett listens to Dinah talking about the past, 'A violence in which some threat, some accusation of betrayal thrashed like a half-glimpsed subterranean monster began to swell in her' (p. 155). The depiction of the characters in this episode incorporates one of the sudden swings in sympathy that contributes to the overall disruptive impact of the text, with its continual shifts in moral and emotional allegiances. For Dinah's progress, like that of several of Rosamond Lehmann's heroines, follows the decline in value-systems that for Lehmann reflects twentieth-century cultural change. In her adoption of fashionable Bohemianism, Dinah, independent, articulate and sexually liberated, embodies the freedoms of her age. Mrs Burkett, on the other hand, a representative of middle-class women of the pre-war era, takes a more tolerant approach to the issues that Dinah insists on proclaiming so stridently – sex, marriage and the problematic nature of personal relations. Her sensibility operates in a different mode from that of her daughter's and her intuitive awareness and level of comprehension appear to transcend Dinah's self-conscious and analytical exposure of private issues.

Whereas Dinah defies propriety and established codes of behaviour, her sister, Madeleine, respects and embraces them. Having married a member of the landed gentry, she accepts bourgeois respectability unquestioningly, and in this picture of two sisters whose lives have taken different directions, Rosamond Lehmann gives shape to the dualism that was contained within a single character in *The Weather in the Streets* and *The Ballad and the Source*. Madeleine is the inheritor of her mother's sensitivity, the conservatism of her way of life no impediment to her capacity for loving. Her longing for stability and her naïve trust in lasting relationships are balanced by Dinah's anti-establishment impulses. Dinah, with no secure career, having frittered her talents on the fringes of the amoral avant-garde, drifts into liaisons that serve only to damage her fragile hold on a unitised self. In the conflict of codes that the two sisters emblematise, each feels alienated from the other, Madeleine in particular becoming the victim of an inferiority complex provoked by her sister's obvious contempt for a style that she has rejected. The reunion with Dinah stimulates angry memories of times when, visiting her sister's flat, she was made to feel that her suburban values, and by extenuation her personality, were discredited and despised by Dinah's free-thinking friends. In a self-regarding pose typical of Lehmann's heroines, Madeleine sees herself through the eyes of others as 'a bungler, a humiliated figure; once again proved unacceptable by Dinah's standards, summed up, contemptuously walked out on by one of this crew, her Betters' (p. 180). Like Mrs Burkett, she too finds difficulty in releasing pent-up emotion. In the scene where she confronts Rickie with evidence of his guilt, her calm demeanour is counteractive, for 'Volcanoes of invective and abuse boiled up in her towards explosion' only to sink down again 'leaving her inert' (p. 131). Madeleine's control over her anger is symptomatic of her powerlessness, just as in *A Note in Music* Grace Fairfax could not give voice to the extremes of despair or joy that afflicted her, her outward placidity functioning as a deceptive screen.

The Echoing Grove gives more direct attention to the emotional turmoil that lies undetected beneath the public mask than any of Lehmann's other works, where it is tempered by changes in tone or by narrative filters that serve to ameliorate its impact. In this novel, however, the raw states of the human psyche are exposed to visible, unrelenting scrutiny. It becomes clear that dialogue is a camouflage, and that language functions as an elaborate sign-system where the words convey only a fraction of the meaning. As Rickie listens to Dinah's curt comments at a crucial moment of revelation in the novel, 'he knew that this was only half of the heart of the matter: that the tone was one she seized on, in pride and fear, when her self-esteem or confidence had received a sudden shock' (p. 99). In intimate relationships men and women are alert to the signals that will decode the real messages. The frequency of broken sentences in the text reveals the failure of words as a tool of communication, and as characters struggle to express or to accommodate their unvoiced traumas, the extent of their isolation is effectively realised. *The Echoing Grove* is a book packed with emotional crises, as characters emit cries for help, cries that, though recognised, are often ignored.

At the heart of the intensive analysis of personal anxieties is Rickie Masters, a man racked with guilt and torn between legality and passion. Like that of the other main characters in this novel, Rickie's portrayal owes a considerable debt to contemporary psychoanalytic theory, in its insistence on the unarticulated fears and stresses that lie beneath social composure. *The Echoing Grove* allows insight into fundamental emotional states – hatred, fear, anxiety, jealousy – and investigates both their realisation and their roots. In the portrait of Rickie as a man under pressure, at the mercy of two conflicting behavioural systems, Lehmann draws a powerful picture of inner tensions and the resulting severe psychological and physiological damage they inflict. The mental anguish that Rickie undergoes as he tries to negotiate his way through the different types of relationship he has established

with Madeleine and Dinah is dramatised through a series of
interior monologues that accentuate the idea of psychic fracture.

> Why, when he had torn open the orange envelope, had his eyes,
> or mind, immediately – done something to the message dancing
> on the flimsy paper – censored it somehow, rejected it? Delay,
> delay. . . . *Severe delay: sudden delay: slight delay: serious
> delay . . . now safe, not safe, now saved* . . . which, which?
> Oh, *destination*, ominous word! Come . . . to the place she had
> reached, where it was appointed that he should come to meet
> her. I knew it all along, he told himself. I sent her to her death,
> her destination; persuading her, himself, that the impossible
> was child's play; that the plot, so monstrous, so plausible,
> devised with such cunning ingenuity, could outsmart the God
> of Wrath. *Punishment. Crime* . . . His hands on the wheel went
> limp, began to shake. *Hate.* (p. 91)

As Rickie drives to Dinah, after receiving the telegram summon-
ing him to her sick-bed, his thoughts lurch wildly in barely
controlled hysteria. His accumulated guilt has complicated
origins, guilt at his association with Dinah, at his betrayal of
Madeleine and at his sense of injustice towards Dinah, whom he
has left to suffer and perhaps die giving birth to his child. The
events, ideas and memories that rush through his mind emanate as
a disordered stream of thought that reproduces his inner chaos.
The novel evokes different degrees of emotional reality, its stylis-
tic range projecting an acute sense of Rickie's mental
deterioration in the re-creation of internal processes. The rhetorical questioning and self-analysis of the above passage, for
instance, give way a few pages later to a more abrupt, but equally
frenzied attempt at self reassurance.

> He came back optimistic to the office at three-thirty, read two
> reports laid on his desk during his absence, couldn't make head
> or tail of them, threw up his window, saw, separated from him
> by a hair's breadth yet worlds, worlds out of reach, blue sky, a
> plump white cloud of May, sun in the streets and people walk-
> ing at peace, enjoying it; saw also – no more, no less horrible –
> a sign he had never noticed before in red glass lettering on the

fourth storey of the building opposite: Uhlmann Trusses Abdominal Belts. He sat down again at the desk and put his head in his hands.

Think things out now. Pretty drunk. He thought hard: truth came to him. (p. 96)

These staccato sentences and broken short phrases are quite different from the rhapsodic, lyrical prose of Rosamond Lehmann's earlier romantic novels. The deliberation involved in mental articulation in this passage dramatises the strain the character is experiencing, the lack of spontaneity emphasising the difficulties of logical process. The linguistic incoherence reflects the fragmentation of both personality and the social order, while the exaggerated sense of objective reality serves to magnify Rickie's personal isolation. His physical collapse from a burst duodenal ulcer demonstrates the body's response to stress, a graphic illustration of the effects of psychological pressure.

As the story evolves we see Rickie subject to the destructive effects of passion. Just as Dinah's role as mistress, existing on the fringes of her lover's life, has effectively eroded her identity, so Rickie too loses his sense of direction as he becomes trapped by the conflicting demands of desire and affection. Going from one woman to the other, he is 'all at sea', unable to combine the diverse aspects of his personality into the coherent self that is consistent with social expectation. In a searing analysis of Rickie's dilemma, Lehmann presents a complicated picture of male sexuality as disorienting and ultimately confused. The lengthy conversation with Georgie that takes up a central position in the novel's structure becomes a form of therapy, as he explains incidents from his past that contribute to his current sense of indeterminacy. The basement in which they shelter from the air-raid acquires the status of an analyst's couch as he confesses to her his bewilderment about women. He remembers occasions when lust strips him of his identity, makes him into 'an automaton, a man-machine, enabled to record but not to correlate, let alone feel, a variety of sensory impressions' (p. 226). His initial response to women is one of terror, together with a tension between instinctive drive and emotional and moral inhibition. Two episodes in the novel reveal Rickie's subliminal homosexuality, yet he refuses to acknowledge his desire for men, insisting, even after his uncomfortable memories of a love-affair with a fellow male undergraduate at Oxford, that, 'I'm not a pansy' (p. 246).

One legacy of Freudian theory, concordant with psychoanalytic practice of the 1950s, was the tendency to see the family as the decisive factor in personality formation. *The Echoing Grove* traces back adult failings to significant childhood episodes for all three main characters. In this context, Rickie emerges as the classic product of a broken home, with an overprotective mother who made excessive demands on him after his father's early death. Forced to shoulder premature responsibility, he developed an unnatural closeness with his mother that has inhibited his later relationships with women. Like others of his generation he emerges as a victim of repressed feeling, and in particular of the ethic of masculinity that forbids open displays of weakness. His humiliating memories of schooldays, when to be discovered weeping was to be the object of derision, return to trouble him, but, in a touching reversal from the macho Rollo Spencer, Rickie admits to Georgie that in relationships, 'I'm always the one to cry' (p. 232). For Rickie, as for the women in this novel, love is 'the infernal grove', a quotation from William Blake which, in Lehmann's version for the title for the book, emphasises the hellish and reverberative nature of passion. Only in fleeting episodes – the brief holiday that Rickie takes with Dinah, the family outing he enjoys with Madeleine and the children – is there any suggestion of the pleasures of love. In presenting sexuality as twisted and damaging, the source of the problems that characters experience, Rosamond Lehmann has moved a long way from the intoxicating romanticism that had characterised *Dusty Answer* twenty-five years earlier.

Lehmann's analysis of family tensions is at its most significant in *The Echoing Grove* in her study of the difficult relationship between Dinah and Madeleine. From this altered perspective, Rickie is not only a victim of his own childhood, but is caught in a complicated web of jealousies that reach back into the history of the Burkett household. Ultimately the connection between the sisters is shown to be more deep-seated and more binding than their love for Rickie or for any other men. At the end of the novel, discarded by or having rejected past lovers, the women recognise that it is their relation to one another that has always been the major determining factor in their lives. In this final section, 'The Early Hours', which moves back to the present and the sisters' reunion, Lehmann brings to a head her examination of the mutual understanding that exists between women, and that has been a constant subject of investigation in her earlier writing. In 1931, in *A Letter to a Sister*, Rosamond Lehmann appealed to a joint past and to shared memories as an avenue to full communication, addressing a sister as the only person who could truly appreciate her understanding of life's significance. In *The Echoing Grove*, at the moment of truth between the sisters, Madeleine observes that, 'It should be drummed into one in youth, the importance of living so as to be able to face one's memories when one's old' (p. 280). Their final late-night conversation enacts precisely that confrontation. Together in the darkness the two women discuss, without animosity, their past and the harrowing three-way relationship that has been responsible for their estrangement but that has also paradoxically drawn them together. Despite the fact that their paths have diverged, Dinah and Madeleine are inextricably bound together, their tussle over Rickie's love merely an extension of the competitive spirit and the need for self-affirmation that was bred in childhood. As Dinah admits, 'Propinquity. Hysteria. Escapism. Sense of failure. Impulse of self-destruction. Me. You. Rickie' (p. 282) are all elements that have contributed to the tangled nature of their peculiar interdependence.

This confessional scene allows Lehmann to present more explicitly than in her earlier novels the uncertainties that women experience regarding their own sexuality, and their need for self-definition in a society where women's roles have undergone significant change. In the anonymity of the night, the sisters discuss their early sexual encounters and Dinah acknowledges that her promiscuity was motivated by fear. The almost clinical realism that characterises the analysis of mental and emotional processes throughout the book is repeated here as the sisters recall the past without either sentimentality or remorse. To some extent Dinah and Madeleine act as mouthpieces for their generation, their own confusions mirroring the uncertainties that surround women in a revised climate of sexual freedom. Dinah's final speech sums up the dilemma. 'I can't help thinking it's particularly difficult to be a woman just at present', she tells Madeleine.

> One feels so transitional and fluctuating. . . . So I suppose do men. I believe we *are* all in flux – that the difference between our grandmothers and us is far deeper than we realize – much more fundamental than the obvious social economic one. Our so-called emancipation may be a symptom, not a cause. (p. 292)

Relating the contemporary identity crisis to cultural phenomena, Rosamond Lehmann redirects attention back towards the social determinants of gender and identity, a constant preoccupation in her previous work. The world of *The Echoing Grove* is thus both deeply personal and highly representative. The characters act out their own unique and tragic story, but they come to embody their generation of lost individuals, their isolation a reflection of the disunity and incoherence of post-war Britain in the 1950s.

The painstaking psychological realism that is brought to bear on the analysis of personality is counterbalanced by the formal patterning of the text, patterning that presents men and women as acting out a classical formula in a revised social context. The almost ritualised movement of the players in the game of sexual and psychological manoeuvres that constitutes *The Echoing Grove* is highly structured and helps to intensify their representative status. 'Death wish. Birth trauma. Narcissism, sadism, masochism: the terms of reference were all available', thinks Madeleine, bitterly reflecting on 'this claustrophobic game' (p. 171) that the characters all seem to engage in in their unremitting introspection. Such psychoanalytic jargon effectively reduces personal identity to a series of clinical tropes, dehumanising as well as demoralising. As the mechanics of the story make clear, formal connections between the characters occur at a number of stages. It is not only the intertwined relations of Madeleine, Dinah and Rickie that seem to conform to an imposed design, but minor characters too are used to reinforce the sense of an intricate web of experience. Rob, for example, first encountered as Dinah's lover, next appearing as a young sailor who stays overnight with

Rickie, and finally shown as having been deeply attracted to Madeleine, suggests a further level to the ramifications of association between the three main actors in the drama. Similarly the young woman who is to marry Madeleine's lover, mentioned only in passing in the closing pages of the story, is also known to Dinah, a further link in the chain that binds the sisters together. The interest in narrative complication, introduced in *The Ballad and the Source*, is developed in *The Echoing Grove* with the direct references to the characters as counters in an elaborate game. '*For so the game is ended That should not have begun*' (p. 100), quotes Rickie to himself, musing on his own position as player in the age-old game of love.

This sense of conformity to an overall design is supported by the symbolic use of everyday objects. The cuff-links, for example, that Rickie leaves behind at Dinah's flat, recur at different stages throughout the story and in the memories of different characters, where they have varying levels of significance. Ultimately they function as an image of Rickie's own split identity and allegiance but, more importantly perhaps, they serve to emphasise the structural cohesion of the text as a whole. This system of formal linkage counteracts the episodic narrative organisation of the novel and its abrupt chronology, and helps to underpin the idea of the cyclical and repetitive nature of human relationships. Technically *The Echoing Grove* has much in common with *The Ballad and the Source*, which also perceives characters and events as subordinate to a self-generating sequence. Whereas the artifice of the earlier novel is an explicit subject, in *The Echoing Grove* it is more restrained, contributing rather to the uneasy balance between painful realism and surreal dissociation that the work produces. The cynicism that pervades *The Echoing Grove*, in its detached view of human beings as anguished victims, ultimately fatalistic about their own isolation, forms a natural sequel to the more subdued sadness that characterised *A Note in Music*. Together these two novels contain both a realism of texture in their depiction of the routines of daily life, and a questioning of that reality through the constant switch in perspective and the movement from exterior to interior scene.

8

Later Works

After the publication of *The Echoing Grove*, Rosamond Lehmann did not write another novel for twenty-three years. Undoubtedly her literary silence was due to the sudden death of her daughter, Sally, from polio in 1958. As she acknowledged in 1984,

> I think it true to say that some dimension of creativity dropped off me, so to speak, when that metanoia occurred after Sally left the Earth. I realized, and still do, that I could never write the kind of novel I had always written.[66]

Instead, the works that followed that loss – her one novel, *A Sea-Grape Tree*, her autobiography, *The Swan in the Evening*, and the mystic writings produced with Cynthia Hill Sandys and Wellesley Tudor Pole – are all in some way a response to her personal tragedy, and a testament to her faith in spiritual recovery. They also show Lehmann, at a late stage in her career, experimenting with artistic form in her search for consolation and for an appropriate means of affirming her new-found optimism. In *The Swan in the Evening* she described her difficulty in finding suitable language to convey her condition of despair and 'the intolerable wrestle with words and meanings' (p. 70) that afflicted her during the period immediately following her bereavement. The isolation that had always been such a conspicuous feature of Rosamond Lehmann's portrayal of her fictional heroines now affected her personally and powerfully as she found that her own feelings of desolation and her subsequent mystical experiences could not adequately be translated into a reliable literary medium. 'I was still moving about in worlds not realized', she recalled ten years after the event, 'And the loneliness of this, the sense of exile, caused a well-nigh total seize-up in such powers of self-expression as I have' (p. 89).

Certainly the harsh realist message that lies at the heart of *The Weather in the Streets*, *The Ballad and the Source* and *The Echoing Grove*, the three novels that most compellingly expose the treachery of romantic love, is succeeded in Rosamond Lehmann's later pieces by ideas of visionary promise. But, in considering these works, it is important to realise that however different they might appear in form from the main body of her output, they develop thematic interests that are also fundamental to the earlier fiction. The quotation that Lehmann had borrowed from Walter Savage Landor to provide the title for her second novel – 'But the present like a note in music is nothing but as it appertains to what is past and what is to come'[67] – was to prove prophetic in terms of offering her a rationale for her final writings, and could indeed serve as an epigraph for her work as a whole. All Rosamond Lehmann's major novels stress the importance of memory, and project an abiding consciousness of historical process, but in *The Swan in the Evening* and *A Sea-Grape Tree* the past and future merge to inform the significance of the present moment with an explicitly metaphysical bias. It is this mystic dimension that has most troubled her recent critics, who find it hard to reconcile what is perceived as an eccentric, if not utterly cranky, view of life with the hard-hitting cynicism of a book such as *The Weather in the Streets*.

Yet Lehmann's writing has consistently affirmed the value of intuition in determining life's significance, and formulated the concept of time as a continuum, with the past operating as a living force on present circumstance. Lehmann's involvement in psychic studies, which had provided her with a positive antidote to her sorrow after Sally's death, can thus be seen as an extension of her readiness to privilege the non-rational in her understanding of temporal experience, a feature that had always characterised her work. The conversation, for instance, that Rebecca holds with the ghostly apparition of Sybil Jardine, in *A Sea-Grape Tree*, becomes more than a figment of an overactive imagination, but is also a celebration of the fact that figures from our past remain with us, and that we can continue to learn from their experience.

The interest in human behaviour as cyclical, increasingly evident in *The Ballad and the Source* and *The Echoing Grove*, evolves in Rosamond Lehmann's final work to reach beyond the normally accepted limits of a life span.

The Swan in the Evening was Rosamond Lehmann's first excursion into authorship after her daughter's death. Subtitled 'Fragments of an Inner Life', it deliberately avoids a systematic sequential structure, its four sections dealing rather with impressionistic episodes, which are only loosely linked by chronology. The book begins conventionally enough with memories of Lehmann's own childhood, but the text then moves abruptly to the moment of Sally's death, and to an almost defensive account of how Lehmann came to terms with this through her belief in survival beyond the grave. The final section is written in the form of a letter to her granddaughter, Anna, justifying the work and its departure from expected norms. Although the recollections are presented as fragmentary with no attempt to impose logical sequence, the work gains coherence through the recurrent motifs of death, betrayal and loss, which gradually build up to create a mood of subdued acquiescence. Lehmann's terror at the thought she might have mistakenly killed her baby brother by giving him perfume to drink; the inconsolable grief of the coachman after his small daughter's death from diphtheria; her own appendicitis; the discovery of a man's body floating in the River Thames: these are the memories of childhood that dominate, memories informed by the sombre understanding of old age. In this work, painful emotions take precedence over the sunny childhood days, and the moments of intense feeling that are so vividly resurrected tend to be those of fear, pity, humiliation and panic. The potential for heartache, which lurked behind the joyous expectancy of *Dusty Answer* and was fully explored in the later novels, is revealed in *The Swan in the Evening* to be deeply rooted in Lehmann's own experience. As she admits, 'Ecstasy, anguish – the violent unpredictability and violence of Janus-headed life: this is the pattern graven on me; smiles, kindness, safe anchorage, turning within an instant to threatened trouble or actual catastrophe' (p. 50). Rosamond Lehmann's novels continually dramatise this unpredictability, the intensity of their conveyed experience always precarious in the potential or actual swings from security to disaster that they incorporate. The irony that underlies her work is crucially reliant on this profound understanding of the double-edged nature of most situations, and Lehmann's ability to communicate this ambivalence is embedded in her own history, which forms, as *The Swan in the Evening* suggests, a pattern of disillusionment and betrayal.

In *The Swan in the Evening*, Rosamond Lehmann presents cameos from her own childhood with episodes from her daughter's life, which then connect to her address to her granddaughter. This interrelationship between three generations of women in a single family focuses attention on the cyclical nature of experience and the legacy to be transmitted from one generation to another, a prominent theme in Lehmann's fictional writings. It is a crucial ingredient in *The Ballad and the Source*, touched on in *The Echoing Grove*, and it reappears in her final novel, *A Sea-Grape Tree*. Childhood invariably carries special meaning in Lehmann's writing. Her child narrators, Judith Earle, Olivia Curtis and Rebecca Landon, have a freshness that endows them with creative power, their very responsiveness to experience invigorating their imaginative capabilities. In *The Swan in the Evening* and *A Sea-Grape Tree* the image of childhood is invested with a further dimension to function as a symbol of future promise. Here the introduction of the visionary element directs attention to childhood, not just as a period when human insight is uncorrupted by social pressure, but as a reminder of the natural and continuous sequence of life's rhythms. In *A Sea-Grape Tree*, Sybil Jardine, the woman who had exerted such fascination over Rebecca as a young girl, returns in spirit as a reminder of 'the source', the female creative force that she has inherited, and in that same novel, the baby girl, Tarni, Sybil's great-granddaughter, appears as a further link in a chain of experience that binds past and future together.

The idea of the cycle can be equally applied to Rosamond Lehmann's own literary career, as the tone of her last works recaptures the optimism that marked her very first novel. The fantasy that Lehmann had once identified as offering a solution to the problems of coping with the uncertainty of post-war conditions dominates *A Sea-Grape Tree* to reassert, in more mellow mood, the idealism of *Dusty Answer*, the novel that had been published almost half a century earlier. In this last book, Rebecca Landon, the character first encountered as a child in *The Ballad and the Source*, reappears as an adult, a young woman battered by an unhappy love-affair. Abandoned by her married lover, she finds solace on a Caribbean island, where she engages in an idyllic love-affair with a man who is also a damaged victim of misguided passion. The setting is pure fantasy, the luxuriant beauty of the desert island creating a dream world remote from the painful social environment that Rebecca has left behind. In the lush tropical paradise, Rebecca can act out the scenario that has eluded other Lehmann heroines: the consummation of perfect love in a carefree ambience. In this and in the atmosphere of promise that suffuses the novel, she reflects the renewed hope of Lehmann's old age. Ten years after the publication of *A Sea-Grape Tree*, Rosamond Lehmann declared that,

> I have come to feel the comedy view of life is greater than the tragic view. I think life is a divine comedy, and – for instance – that *The Tempest* is the greatest of Shakespeare's works: written, presumably, when all the personal agony is over, and can be looked at with detachment and serenity.[68]

In transmitting that feeling of serenity, *A Sea-Grape Tree* provides a fitting coda for the emotional turbulence and harsh social analysis that are the hallmarks of Lehmann's main body of work.

Significantly, in this last novel, Rebecca is introduced without a name, her true identity revealed only gradually. Her anonymity establishes her as the prototype of the essential Rosamond Lehmann heroine, that passionate individual whose longing can find no adequate complement in the fraught society of the modern world. The child who was Rebecca in *The Ballad and the Source* has grown into a woman whose aimless existence can only find its true direction in the fulfilment of her romantic desires, and in this she resembles Lehmann's other creations, Judith, Grace, Olivia, Sybil and Dinah. The growth of twentieth-century feminism that nominally allows women to develop an independent existence has, for Lehmann's women, a doubly frustrating aspect. On the one hand it facilitates the release and expression of the libido, but it also confronts them forcibly with the fact of their reliance on other individuals, and, in the expression of hetero-sexual love, with their inability to free themselves from the patriarchal structures that they both respond to and resent. For Lehmann's heroines have an emotional and erotic centre that requires permanent sustenance. They can find no contentment in the domestic or professional tasks which occupy the daily round, but come alive only in the vitalisation of their inner being, their sexuality the stimulus that provides them with definition. While the heroines of Lehmann's earlier novels devote their energies to passionate affairs that either fail to materialise or prove to be deficient, Rebecca's discovery of love in *A Sea-Grape Tree* results from the aftermath of disappointment, and her ultimate happiness is made the more poignant by her understanding and experience of suffering. In this she completes the structure of euphoria and disillusionment that forms the basis of the Lehmann woman's experience.

A Sea-Grape Tree forms a sequel to *The Ballad and the Source*, a book that deals with the thwarting of natural processes, and as one critic has remarked, cannot be comprehended before reading its predecessor.[69] As well as showing the harmonious completion to the saga of a family at war within itself, the novel illuminates another topic that is of permanent interest in Lehmann's writing, that of artistic creativity. Both *The Ballad and the Source* and *A Sea-Grape Tree* open with Rebecca Landon being told stories about the past, and in both works Rebecca is presented as a catalyst, an inspirational force who generates events around her. In this, she, like Olivia Curtis in *Invitation to the Waltz*, fulfils Lehmann's definition of the function of the author as a passive instrument, a view propounded in essays as well as in a number of her fictional works. Yet Lehmann's characters belie their apparent passivity, and their dynamism is demonstrated in their ability to create substance from minimal materials. Like Rosamond Lehmann herself, Rebecca, Olivia, Judith and Grace are heroines who are active in generating imaginative worlds, their constructions revealing a level of experience beyond that of external observation. In her essay, 'The Future of the Novel', Lehmann suggests an association between the act of narrative and a feminine principle of creativity. Commenting on genesis as 'the image, or isolated images which have become embedded in the

mass of accumulated material in the author's "centre"', she observes how 'when the moment comes (it cannot be predicted, but
can be helped on by the right kind of passivity) these images will
start to become pregnant, to illuminate one another, to condense
and form hitherto unsuspected relationships'.[70] As one critic has
noted, this 'connection between creative writing on the one hand,
and sexuality and maternity on the other, goes deeper than mere
analogy. They all derive from the same source, the uncon-
scious.'[71]

This notion of an author as a receptive screen who filters images and allows them to coalesce into meaningful shape should
not blind us to Lehmann's meticulous approach to the craft of
writing, and to the status she consequently accorded narrative as
a subject in her work. From *Dusty Answer* onwards, Lehmann's
heroines are inventive artists who also need discipline to channel
and express their excess of sensitive awareness effectively. In the
1950s Lehmann inveighed against contemporary authors whose
work seemed to her to epitomise sloppy practice:

> Why do they use words so crudely, with so complacent an
> indifference to their quality, with such lack of love for them?
> Why don't they bother to master the rudiments of grammar?
> Why don't they learn to write better by reading more widely
> and more diligently and with more sense of proportion and per-
> spective?[72]

Her remark reveals much about her own artistic practice, her
informed position and her sense of literary composition as
deliberate and highly fashioned. Her own interest in formal
experiment is apparent in virtually all her novels from *A Note in
Music* onwards, and the reflexivity of *The Ballad and the Source*
and *The Echoing Grove* in particular draws specific attention to
her conviction that art is a vital means of shaping and interpreting
human experience.

Rosamond Lehmann has often been dismissed as a 'feminine'
novelist, a term that was used pejoratively to imply limitations in
scope and interests. In the revised contemporary critical climate,
however, and the insights afforded by feminist literary theory, it
has become possible to read Lehmann's distinctively female slant

as a mark of her achievement rather than a defect. Certainly her work takes the emotional lives of women as a central subject, but in exploring the nature of the female psyche, her fiction also exposes the dilemma of twentieth-century individuals, caught in a culture that appears to liberate but in fact imprisons them. Lehmann's heroines, combining an intellectual with a romantic temperament, are definitively products of the modern world, and their stories of vulnerability and dislocation reflect the cultural crisis of an England recovering from the shock of two world wars. For in her view of women's experience, Lehmann is also an acute social historian, a bitter analyst of the British class system and of its impact on gender and identity. Individual women thus provide a locus for a wholescale investigation of the interrelated issues of history, culture and personality as they affect modern society. History on both a personal and a national level is a pivotal subject of enquiry in Rosamond Lehmann's fiction, her men and women subject to the forces of cultural change that determines their fates. Her first works, *Dusty Answer*, *A Note in Music*, *Invitation to the Waltz* and *The Weather in the Streets*, are, to a considerable extent, a response to the Great War and its radical invasion into an established way of life. The second-wave writing, *The Ballad and the Source*, *The Echoing Grove* and the short stories, written during and after the Second World War, reflect the tremors of renewed social instability of that period. Although *The Ballad and the Source* looks back to the time of the First World War, it does so from a position of revised knowledge, offering a historical perspective on a world that has gone for ever. In her satire and exposé of established power structures, Lehmann makes it clear that sexual politics remain a fraught issue in the twentieth century, despite the superficial changes that the two wars have brought about.

In her relatively limited output – only seven novels in fifty years of active composition – Lehmann manages to suggest not only the forces and nature of cultural change as they affect her protagonists, but also an ambivalence towards this process that is profoundly unsettling. Rosamond Lehmann is an author whose work is full of tensions and contradictions. In *The Swan in the Evening* she confessed that in her own life 'rectitude, stern puritanic principles inculcated by my mother strove ever with an

ardent, pleasure-enjoying, love-hungry nature' (p. 69). This tension between control and licence is present in all her novels, and
contributes to her view of the problematic relationship between
individuals and their communities. Her heroines long for the
security of home, of the past and of family structures, but they
also rebel against that restriction which inhibits the full expression of passionate abandon. The radicalism of Rosamond
Lehmann's early writing, which so shocked the readership of the
1920s, never fully subsided. It remained in uneasy partnership
with a conservatism that continued to speak for the political
indeterminacy that has characterised twentieth-century Britain.
Lehmann's greatest achievement rests in her ability to dramatise
this ambivalence and to expose the ways in which it threatens and
determines the nature of individual, and particularly female,
experience in modern culture.

Notes

1. Rosamond Lehmann, *The Swan in the Evening* (London: Virago Press, 1982) p. 65.

2. Cecil Day Lewis, 'An Italian Visit: Part Six: Elegy Before Death: At Settignano', *Collected Poems* (London: Weidenfeld & Nicolson, 1954) p. 349.

3. Lehmann, *The Swan in the Evening*, op. cit., p. 9.

4. Bel Mooney, 'Lost Loves of a Soul Survivor: The Times Profile: Rosamond Lehmann', *The Times*, 9 February 1984.

5. Janet Watts, 'Rosamond Lehmann', in *Writing Lives: Conversations Between Women Writers*, ed. Mary Chamberlain (London: Virago Press, 1988) p. 151.

6. Ibid.

7. Lehmann, *The Swan in the Evening*, op. cit., p. 65.

8. Mooney, 'Lost Loves', op. cit.

9. Sandra M. Gilbert and Susan Gubar, *No Man's Land: The Place of the Woman Writer in the Twentieth Century*, vol. 2: *Sexchanges* (New Haven, Conn.: Yale University Press, 1989) p. 263.

10. Lehmann, *The Swan in the Evening*, op. cit., p. 68

11. Rosamond Lehmann, *Rosamond Lehmann's Album* (London: Chatto & Windus, 1985) p. 53.

12. Mooney, 'Lost Loves', op. cit.

13. Alfred Noyes, *The Sunday Times*, 22 May 1927.

14. Stephen Spender, *World Within World* (London: Hamish Hamilton, 1951) p. 143

15. Lehmann, *Rosamond Lehmann's Album*, op. cit., p. 100.

16. Rosamond Lehmann, *The Gypsy's Baby* (London: Virago Press, 1982) p. 57

17. Sean Day Lewis, *C. Day Lewis: A Literary Life* (London: Weidenfeld & Nicolson, 1980) pp. 143–4.

18. Lehmann, *Rosamond Lehmann's Album*, op. cit., p. 107.

19. Ibid., p. 107.

20. Lehmann, *The Swan in the Evening*, op. cit., pp. 68–9.

21. Ibid., p. 69.

22. Virginia Woolf, 'Mr Bennett and Mrs Brown', *Collected Essays*, vol. 1 (London: Chatto & Windus, 1966) p. 320.

23. For further critical comment, see, among others, Malcolm Bradbury, *Possibilities* (London: Oxford University Press, 1973); David Daiches, *The Novel and the Modern World* (Chicago: Chicago University Press, 1960); Douglas Hewitt, *English Fiction of the Early Modern Period* (London & New York: Longman, 1988).

24. Malcolm Bradbury, 'The Novel in the 1920s', in *The Sphere History of Literature in the English Language*, vol. 7, ed. Bernard Bergonzi (London: Sphere Books, 1970) p. 181.

25. Malcolm Bradbury, *The Modern World: Ten Great Writers* (Harmondsworth, Middx.: Penguin Books, 1989).

26. Patricia Waugh, *Feminine Fictions: Revisiting the Post-Modern* (London: Routledge, 1989) p. 71.

27. Virginia Woolf, *A Room of One's Own* (Harmondsworth, Middx.: Penguin Books, 1945) p. 96.

28. *The Diary of Virginia Woolf*, vol. III, ed. Anne Olivier Bell (London: Hogarth Press, 1980) pp. 314–15.

29. Virginia Woolf, *A Room of One's Own*, op. cit., p. 76.

30. Rachel Blau DuPlessis, *Writing Beyond the Ending: Narrative Strategies of Twentieth-Century Women Writers* (Bloomington: University of Indiana Press, 1985) p. 4.

31. Rosalind Miles, *The Fiction of Sex: Themes and Function of Sex Difference in the Modern Novel* (London: Vision Press, 1974) p. 123.

32. Waugh, *Feminine Fictions*, op. cit., p77.

33. For example, Sandra M. Gilbert and Susan Gubar, *The Madwoman in the Attic: The Woman Writer and the Nineteenth-Century Literary Imagination* (New Haven, Conn.: Yale University Press, 1979); Judith Lowder Newton, *Women, Power and Subversion: Social Strategies in British Fiction 1778–1860* (London: Methuen, 1981); Mary Poovey, *The Proper Lady and the Woman Writer* (Chicago: University of Chicago Press, 1984).

34. Gillian Hanscombe and Virginia Smythe, *Writing for their Lives: The Modernist Woman 1910–1940* (London: The Women's Press, 1987) p. 7.

35. Ibid., p. 8.

36. Katherine Mansfield, *Journal and Letters*, ed. C. K. Stead (Harmondsworth, Middx.: Penguin Books, 1977) p. 225.

37. See Diana E. LeStourgeon, *Rosamond Lehmann* (New York: Twayne, 1965) for a summary of these attitudes.

38. Mary McCarthy, *On the Contrary* (1962), quoted in Miles, *The Fiction of Sex*, op. cit., pp. 275–6.

39. Hanscombe and Smythe, *Writing for their Lives*, op. cit.

40. Nancy Armstrong, *Desire and Domestic Fiction* (New York: Oxford University Press, 1987) p. 57.

41. Dorothy Richardson, *Pilgrimage* (London: Virago Press, 1979) vol. 2, p. 251.

42. Woolf, *A Room of One's Own*, op. cit., pp. 81–2.

43. Violet Trefusis, *Broderie Anglaise* (London: Methuen, 1987) p. 101.

44. Gilbert and Gubar, *Sexchanges*, op. cit., p. 303.

45. George Dangerfield, 'Rosamond Lehmann and the Perilous Enchantment of Things Past', *The Bookman*, February 1933, p. 173.

46. G. E. Moore, *Principia Ethica* (Cambridge: Cambridge University Press, 1903).

47. Gilbert and Gubar, *Sexchanges*, op. cit., p. 301.

48. Hugh Kenner, *A Sinking Island: The Modern English Writers* (London: Barrie & Jenkins, 1988) p. 161.

49. Dangerfield, 'Rosamond Lehmann', op. cit., p. 172.

50. D. H. Lawrence, *Women in Love* (Harmondsworth, Middx.: Penguin Books, 1960) p. 261.

51. John Berger, 'Ways of Seeing', *The Listener*, 20 January, 1972.

52. 'The Beauty System', quoted in Nancy Armstrong and Leonard Tennenhouse, *The Ideology of Conduct* (London: Methuen, 1987) p. 17.

53. 'H.C.H.', review of *The Trap, The Calendar of Modern Letters*, June 1925, pp. 328–9, in Randall Stevenson, *The British Novel since the Thirties: An Introduction* (London: Batsford, 1986) p. 16.

54. Janice A. Radway, *Reading the Romance: Women, Patriarchy and Popular Literature* (London: Verso Press, 1987) p. 212.

55. As for instance argued by Jan Cohn, *Romance and the Erotics of Property: Mass Market Fiction for Women* (Durham, NC: Duke University Press, 1988); Carol Thurston, *The Romance Revolution* (Chicago: University of Illinois Press, 1988); and Radway, *Reading the Romance*, op. cit.

56. Lehmann, 'Rosamond Lehmann Reading', in 'New Soundings' by John Lehmann, *New World Writing*, no. 2, 1952, p. 48.

57. Watts, *Writing Lives*, op. cit., p. 156.

58. Lehmann, *The Swan in the Evening*, op. cit., p. 22.

59. Ibid., p. 65.

60. Lehmann, *New World Writing*, op. cit., p. 48.

61. Lehmann, *The Gypsy's Baby*, p. 57.

62. Lilian Feder, *Ancient Myth in Modern Poetry* (Princeton, NJ: Princeton University Press, 1971) p. 407, quoted in Sydney Janet Kaplan, 'Rosamond Lehmann's *The Ballad and the Source*: A Confrontation with "The Great Mother"', *Twentieth Century Literature*, vol. 27, no. 2, Summer 1981.

63. Nancy Chodorow, *The Reproduction of Mothering: Psychoanalysis and the Sociology of Gender* (Berkeley: University of California Press, 1978).

64. Rosamond Lehmann, 'The Future of the Novel?', *Britain Today*, no. CXII, June 1946, p. 7.

65. Walter Allen, *Tradition and Dream* (London: Phoenix House, 1954) p. 196.

66. Interview with Mooney, 'Lost Loves', op. cit.

67. Walter Savage Landor, *Imaginary Conversations*, vol. I (London: J. M. Dent, 1891) pp. 16–17.

68. Watts, *Writing Lives*, op. cit., p. 159.

69. Janet Watts, 1982 introduction to the new edition of *A Sea-Grape Tree* (London: Virago Press, 1985) p. xi.

70. Lehmann, 'The Future of the Novel?', op. cit., pp. 9–10.

71. Sydney Janet Kaplan, *Feminine Consciousness in the Modern British Novel* (Chicago: University of Illinois Press, 1975) p. 113.

72. Lehmann, *New World Writing*, op. cit., p. 49.

Select Bibliography

NOTES ON EDITIONS

In this book, references are to the Virago Press editions of Rosamond Lehmann's novels, except for the following: *Dusty Answer*, Penguin Books; *The Echoing Grove*, Penguin Books; *A Letter to a Sister*, Hogarth Press. Place of publication is London unless otherwise stated.

WORKS BY ROSAMOND LEHMANN

Novels

Dusty Answer (1927; New York, 1927).
A Note in Music (1930; New York, 1930).
Invitation to the Waltz (1932; New York, 1932).
The Weather in the Streets (1936; New York, 1936).
The Ballad and the Source (1944; New York, 1945).
The Echoing Grove (1953; New York, 1953).
A Sea-Grape Tree (1976; New York, 1967).

Short stories

The Gypsy's Baby and Other Stories (1946; New York, 1946).
'A Hut, a Sea-Grape Tree', in *Winter's Tales*, vol. 2 (Macmillan, 1956; New York, 1956).

Autobiography

The Swan in the Evening: Fragments of an Inner Life (1967; New York, 1967).
Rosamond Lehmann's Album (Chatto & Windus, 1985).

Play

No More Music (1939; New York, 1939).

Other non-fiction

A Letter to a Sister (1931; New York, 1932).
A Man Seen Afar (with Wellesley Tudor Pole) (Spearman, 1965).
Letters from our Daughters (with Cynthia Hill Sandys) (College of Psychic Studies, 1972).
The Awakening Letters, ed. Rosamond Lehmann and Cynthia Hill Sandys (Spearman, 1978).

Translations

Jacques Lemarchand, *Geneviève* (1947).
Jean Cocteau, *Children of the Game* (1955; republished as *The Holy Terrors*, New York, 1957).

Selected articles

'Books in General', *New Statesman and Nation*, no. 29, 3 March 1945.
'The Future of the Novel?', *Britain Today*, no. 122, June 1946.
'Miss Rosamond Lehmann', *New Statesman and Nation*, no. 47, 30 January 1954.
'Rosamond Lehmann Reading', in John Lehmann, 'New Soundings', *New World Writing*, no. 2, 1952.

Selected interviews

Janet Watts, 'Rosamond Lehmann' in Mary Chamberlain (ed.), *Writing Lives: Conversations between Women Writers* (Virago Press, 1988).
Bel Mooney, 'Lost Loves of a Soul Survivor', *The Times*, 9 February 1984, p. 8.

SELECTED CRITICISM

John Atkins, 'Rosamond Lehmann', in *Six Novelists Look at Society: An Enquiry into the Social Views of Elizabeth Bowen, L. P. Hartley, Rosamond Lehmann, Christopher Isherwood, Nancy Mitford, C. P. Snow* (Calder, 1977).
Panthea Reid Broughton, 'Narrative License in *The Echoing Grove*', *South Central Review*, no. 1, 1984, pp. 85–107.
Sean Day Lewis, *C. Day Lewis: An English Literary Life* (Weidenfeld & Nicolson, 1980).

Wiktoria Dorosz, 'Subjective Vision and Human Relationships in the Novels of Rosamond Lehmann', *Studia Anglistica Upsaliena*, no. 23 (Stockholm: Acta Universitatis Upsaliensis, 1975).

James Gindin, 'Rosamond Lehmann: A Revaluation', *Contemporary Literature*, vol. 15, 1974, pp. 203–11.

Margaret T. Gustafson, 'Rosamond Lehmann: A Bibliography', *Twentieth Century Literature*, vol. 4, no. 4, 1959, pp. 143–7.

Sydney Janet Kaplan, 'Rosamond Lehmann', in *Feminine Consciousness in the Modern British Novel* (Chicago: University of Illinois Press, 1975).

Sydney Janet Kaplan, 'Rosamond Lehmann's *The Ballad and the Source*: A Confrontation with "The Great Mother"', *Twentieth Century Literature*, vol. 27, no. 2, 1987, pp. 127–45.

Diana E. LeStourgeon, *Rosamond Lehmann* (New York: G. K. Hall, Twayne, 1965).

Vida Markovic, 'Mrs Jardine', in *The Changing Face: Disintegration of Personality in the Twentieth-Century British Novel 1900–1950* (Carbondale: Southern Illinois University Press, 1970).

Judy Simons, 'The Torment of Loving: The Inter-war Novels of Rosamond Lehmann', in *Writers of the Old School: British Novelists of the 1930s*, ed. Janice Rossen (Macmillan, 1992).

Lawrence Thornton, 'The Ballad and the Source', *Virginia Woolf Quarterly*, Fall 1972.

Gillian Tindall, *Rosamond Lehmann: An Appreciation* (Chatto & Windus, 1984).

Index